LISTEN SOFTLY

LISTEN SOFTLY

A PARENT'S GUIDE TO DISCOVERING TEEN STRENGTHS, BUILDING BONDS, AND INSPIRING ACTION

KATHLEEN SABO

THE PAPER HOUSE
PUBLISHING

CONTENTS

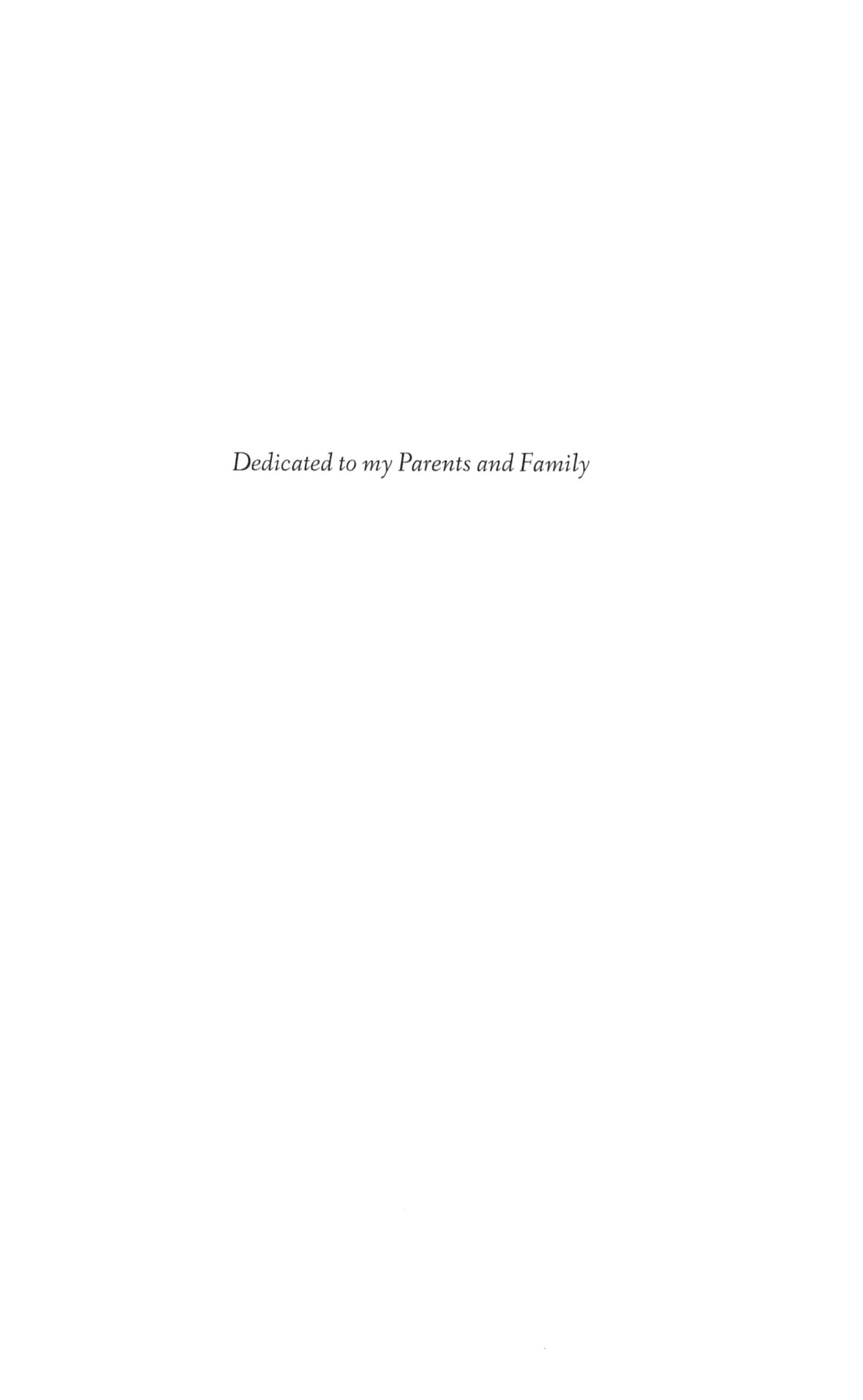

Dedicated to my Parents and Family

INTRODUCTION

In "Listen Softly: A Parent's Guide to Discovering Teen Strengths, Building Bonds, and Inspiring Action," we dive into an exploration of love, deepening our understanding of both us and our teens. This book teaches us a unique way of listening that not only helps us comprehend our own emotions but also clarifies what truly matters to us. This approach enhances our parenting by ensuring our decisions are heart driven.

Listening softly does more than aid our personal growth. It also fosters a connection with something larger, like faith or spirituality. Such connections can offer strength and comfort, especially when facing challenges with teens.

Presenting a parenting philosophy centered on attentiveness and inner wisdom, this book introduces the Inner Connection Quest, a transformative journey that promotes personal enrichment and individual progress. The approach encourages a fresh perspective on our teens, fostering their independence while ensuring our support remains steadfast. Embracing this path teaches us that the finest guidance often comes from listening softly, allowing us to filter out distractions and tune into the wisdom of our hearts and souls. Such a process not only deepens our understanding but also bolsters confidence in our parenting abilities.

Ultimately, the Inner Connection Quest enhances our awareness, builds our inner resilience, and leads to greater happiness. We learn that the answers we're looking for are already inside us. Through stories, reflections, and practical experiences, this book offers a roadmap for nurturing the inner connection within us and with our teens. This can turn parenting into an adventure of hope, love, and deep bonds. It's about finding the beauty in being a parent and loving our kids in the best way possible.

My journey began within a faith community, but I soon realized the path is much broader. At first, I was eager for others to join my religious group, hoping they'd find the same insights. But I've learned that everyone's journey to understanding is personal, guided by their own experiences and inner voice. This deep, personal connection is what this book is all about.

The intention isn't to dictate beliefs or to understand the world in a specific way. Instead, it's about feeling an overwhelming sense of love and delight. This epiphany came to me during a discussion on Adam and Eve when I was a teen. Prior to that, I struggled with the relationships I saw among my peers, specifically the way that my friends were seeking happiness through romantic relationships, drugs, and parties. I knew that was not the way for me to find fulfillment, but I didn't know why. It seemed like I was not normal.

The experience I had in a spiritual seminar I attended cannot be explained in words. It was a feeling and a calling of sorts. There was a force of internal strength that reached deep inside of me. It changed my life in the way that I felt motivation and direction. This wasn't a one-time experience, but it initiated a course of living with purpose. This perspective has transformed how I view life, infusing it with meaning.

My work with the Universal Peace Federation,[1] along with my travels, initiatives, and studies in human development, have all helped shape me. Like your unique experiences and strong points have made you who you are, my journey has made me who I am today.

I've had periods of questioning the world and finding transformative solutions for my children during their younger years. Homeschooling was our choice, not because it was the only way, but because it felt suitable for us. I wanted my kids to feel this inner connection. This led me to develop the "Life Goals Approach" and offer it through my Uplifting Education program online. This began in the early 2000s and evolved until the 2020s.

At the heart of the "Life Goals Approach" is helping teens grow and develop. The first goal is guiding kids to see their unique qualities and how these traits can have an influence on the world. This stage is about how teens can recognize their value.

For the second life goal, we focus on building wholesome relationships. Here, we guide kids on the importance of empathy and how their actions affect others. It is about showing teens the strength found in deep connections and how these relationships open up possibilities and enrich everyone involved.

The third life goal is to make a difference in the wider community. This part of the journey is about inspiring teens to contribute positively, offering their talents and character traits to help others.

Just recently, I added to this understanding of life. A simple question about goals and the discussion it sparked in a Facebook group made me realize I needed to think deeper about how we educate teens. This led to the development of the Inner Connection Quest. My goal has always been to lift up and love teens, sharing the powerful sentiments of love, hope, joy, and peace with them.

Inner intelligence is a guide we can all tune into by asking the right questions. I hope this book brings a positive shift to your life and your family's. I've had my doubts in parenting, feared for my children's future, and held regrets for not handling situations well at times. Yet, I discovered we all have the ability to love, forgive, and find hope. Everyone has a unique inner light and love to share.

This book builds upon the Life Goals Approach I developed during my homeschooling years, delving deeper into how our thoughts and the energy they create influence our relationships and our interactions with the world around us.

Bringing a child into this world calls us to undertake more than we ever imagined, involving countless tasks and continuous care. As our children grow into teenagers, this role evolves dramatically, challenging us to expand beyond our current perceptions of our capabilities. What questions, then, should we be asking ourselves? This book doesn't hand out answers. Instead, it aims to spark our own quest for understanding, motivating us to reach our personal best and fullest potential.

Change requires more than tactics. It requires us to discover universal truths from within ourselves. This internal shift transforms our interactions with the world, leading to organic change. In parenting, this means embracing unconditional love and looking beyond surface behaviors to recognize and connect with a teen's true self.

When teens are unsure of themselves or struggling, we can show them we believe in their inherent strengths and their ability to achieve well-being and harmony. This book invites readers to explore their inner capabilities, defined not by past circumstances or future concerns but by the choices we make in the present. By tuning into our inner voice and following its direction, we can ignite the spark of insight within ourselves.

I've filled this book with practical advice and insights to help enhance your journey through parenting. Plus, I've included a collection of additional resources and tools on a special website just for you at https://www.upliftingeducation.com/resources. On this resource page you will also find a community where we can keep the discussion going.

Are you ready for an amazing journey? Welcome to the Inner Connection Quest, a unique approach to parenting that emphasizes nurturing teens' inner growth.

This book aims to transform the teen years from a potentially stressful and confusing time into an exploration, preparing them for a life filled with meaning and happiness. Let's begin this adventure together and discover where it leads us!

PART ONE
GROWTH AND DEVELOPMENT

On our journey with the Inner Connection Quest, we begin by enhancing our strengths. We observe how our choices affect everything around us, fostering growth in ourselves and those we care about. This adventure teaches us to understand others, recover from setbacks, and be honest with ourselves. At its heart, it involves calming our busy minds and listening carefully so that wisdom can guide both parents and teens toward what truly matters. By embracing this approach, we learn to grow stronger and connect more deeply.

JOURNEY OF GROWTH AND CONNECTION

JENNA SAT IN THE PASSENGER SEAT OF HER MOTHER'S CAR. HER breath was short and fast, even though she didn't realize it. Her mother noticed, though.

"Don't worry, sweetheart," Angela said, casting a fleeting glance at her daughter. "You're really good. Others will see it also."

Jenna managed a feeble smile, unwilling to confess the depth of her fear. She was haunted by the thought that people might critique her writing harshly. However, an inner voice fought those thoughts by echoing her mother's words.

As they entered the parking lot, Jenna's eyes widened. The workshop was nestled in a rustic brick building. Several others, apparently headed to the workshop, walked toward the building. Angela found an available spot.

Jenna took a deep breath, her heart a flutter of nerves and excitement. She caught her mom's warm, encouraging smile. "You've got this," Angela said, her voice brimming with confidence.

Jenna nodded, took another breath, and barely said, "Kay," in a whisper.

. . .

Nurturing Potential

Parenting teens is like going through a maze together. It's a big adventure for them as they move from being kids to becoming adults, and we're right there with them. I remember my own teen years as a confusing mix of paths. My parents stood by their gazes laden with both hope and apprehension, silently yearning for a guide to navigate this complex maze.

This is where the Inner Connection Quest comes in. Think of it as having a GPS that changes as you need it. With this approach, we don't have to check on teens at every single turn. Instead, we find the best times to talk and connect. It could be a quiet talk before bed, a catch-up once a week, or just a chat when it feels right. These moments light up the way for both parents and teens, helping us see where to go next.

Imagine teens as artists standing in front of a blank canvas. Every choice they make is like a brush stroke on that canvas, gradually painting the picture of their future. We, as parents, provide the paint and brushes, maybe suggest a shade here or a technique there, but the final picture is all theirs, filled with the colors of their dreams and passions.

Like many teens, Jenna explored her passions, trying to find where her interests lay. Just as Angela had identified and nurtured Jenna's enthusiasm, I, too, sought opportunities for my teens. When my daughter was interested in art, I introduced her to a local artist who offered painting classes in her converted garage. This new experience added more colors to her palette and boosted her confidence in her own creativity.

When she became fascinated with horses, she started volunteering at a horse management program. It was a whole new section of the maze for her, where she learned not just about riding but also about caring for these animals. Her commitment and skill grew, leading to opportunities to teach others and turning her passion into a defining part of her journey.

These stories highlight the beauty of guiding teens through the maze, illuminating paths to their passions, and watching as they navigate their way to their unique futures. It's a journey filled with discovery, growth, and connection, where every turn can lead to a new adventure.

———

The sun had already disappeared beneath the horizon, painting the sky in hues of deep purples and blues when Jenna emerged from the creative writing workshop. Angela glanced up from the book she was reading in the car to see her walking at a slow, Eeyore-like pace. Jenna's cheeks were blushed red. Her demeanor immediately set off alarms inside Angela, and the need to comfort her daughter burned strong. She held back and let Jenna get into the car.

As they drove, she cast sidelong glances at her daughter, noting the slump of Jenna's shoulders and the distant look in her eyes. This was the stormy silence that usually preceded Jenna's emotional outbursts. She had to tread carefully. Another couple of minutes passed before she finally said, "What happened, sweetheart? You seem upset."

Jenna's lower lip trembled as she said, "I'm a failure."

Angela took a deep breath, her heart aching with her daughter's distress. She reached over, squeezing Jenna's hand reassuringly. "Why do you say that?"

Jenna looked away but didn't move her hand from the comfort. "No one likes my story."

"Oh honey, I don't think that's true. But what happened?"

"I don't know," she said. "They didn't like it."

They sat silently for a while; she knew Jenna would eventually explain.

"There's one girl," she finally said. "She was so annoying. She acted like she knew everything. Told me my story was all over the place, the characters weren't realistic, and the plot was missing action."

"Seriously?" her mom replied.

"Yeah, but what she said is true."

She squeezed her hand, "I know, sweetheart, I know. Criticism is hard."

Jenna's sleeve went to her eye, wiping a tear. Angela gave another squeeze and said, "You have your unique style. Your writing and your stories have heart. They reflect you. And that's what matters. Never forget that."

The following week, there was another beautiful sunset as Angela again looked up from her book to see Jenna exit the workshop. This time, she walked at a faster pace and even said, "Hey," as she entered the car.

"Not bad," was her response to how it went that day. During that drive home, she explained to Jenna her experience as a painter. She talked about how every writer and artist has their fair share of struggles and failures and how these trials become stepping stones to success.

She came out with a huge smile in the third week. The entire ride home, she rambled excitedly about how her story was evolving.

Week after week, Angela listened to Jenna explain how her stories were improving and how the critiques didn't sting as much anymore. Instead, they got her excited about how to improve her story. Through this experience, she emerged stronger and more determined than ever to be a writer.

Mixing Heart and Mind

Imagine you're in your kitchen about to make a fantastic smoothie. Think of emotions as those juicy, colorful fruits bursting with flavor and life. Now, logic? That's your blender with the characteristics of practical, dependable, and ready to go.

Imagine just munching on a piece of fruit. It's great, right? Pure emotion is raw and wonderful. And then there's the blender, all set but doing nothing much on its own. True magic happens when you toss the fruit in with the blender. Mixing the fruits' lively flavors with the blender's steady rhythm whips up a smoothie that's both delicious and nourishing.

This is much like what happens when teens figure out how to balance their emotions with logic. It's about them finding their way in a world where the energy of their feelings meets the vibe of rational thought. This combo leads to choices that are not just smart but also resonate on a deeper level.

Now, let's talk about that special something—inner wisdom. Imagine it as that secret sauce, maybe a dash of cinnamon or a drizzle of honey that transforms a good smoothie into an unforgettable one. This secret ingredient is subtle, not as in-your-face as the fruit or as mechanical as the blender, but it's what makes the smoothie stand out. It highlights the best of all the other ingredients.

This secret sauce is like the inner wisdom we all carry. That soft, guiding voice somehow knows what's best, even when the world's noise tries to drown it out. It's about trusting that gut feeling, that nudge, helping teens to blend their thoughts and feelings into choices that aren't just okay but great.

Encouraging teens to listen to that inner guidance helps them create decisions that aren't just a balance of heart and head but are also deeply personal. Like adding a unique twist to a smoothie, decisions they make can be infused with their own inner wisdom, making their path through life not just richer but uniquely theirs.

There was a time when my son was all about baseball. He loved it, but for some reason, things weren't clicking on the field. Each missed catch seemed to chip away at his confidence. The obvious move would've been more practice, a new coach, or a good old pep talk to lift his spirits. But life has taught me that pushing harder isn't the only way to grow. Sometimes, what you really need is to see things in a new light to get that spark back.

So, we tried something different. Instead of heading out for more drills, we settled into the comfort of our kitchen with hot cocoa in hand, diving into stories about baseball legends. But we didn't focus on their wins. We talked about the tough times they faced and how they got through them. This wasn't about stepping away from baseball. It was about showing my son that obstacles are part of every journey.

This heart-to-heart wasn't just talk. It was our own Inner Connection Quest. It helped us see the difficulties not as separate moments but as parts of a bigger story. By sharing these stories, I wanted to give my son a fresh way to look at his baseball journey and life itself.

The aim was to create a space where it was okay to be yourself, where every unique story, including his, was celebrated. This approach was about more than baseball. It was about helping him see his value, understand that it's okay to make mistakes, and know that each stumble is a chance to learn.

Returning to our earlier chat about blending emotions and logic with a sprinkle of personal wisdom, this shift in how we approached baseball was like finding that perfect mix. It wasn't just about mixing the right ingredients but about adding our own stories to the blend, making the lessons richer and more meaningful.

Sharing these moments with my son reminded me of the beauty of taking a step back and looking at the bigger picture. It's a reminder for all of us raising teens that sometimes, the best way to help them shine isn't by doing more of what's expected but by sharing and valuing our experiences together. Through empathy and celebrating each person's unique path, we're not just teaching them about a sport or a subject. We're guiding them on how to manage life with confidence and grace.

Journeying Together

At the heart of parenting is the Inner Connection Quest. This approach highlights the importance of personal growth, strong relationships and positively impacting the world around us. But let's be honest, navigating this path can sometimes seem like trying to find our way through a thick forest.

Amid the storm of teenage mood swings, sleepless nights, and never-ending requests, it's easy to lose sight of our purpose and question our impact on this vast journey. Sometimes, the challenges of parenting can overshadow our inner guide.

How did I find my way? By adopting a couple of simple yet powerful practices. Every morning, I took a moment to set a clear intention for the day. As the evening rolled in, I'd practice gratitude, appreciating the day's achievements, no matter how small. Then, I thought about what I wanted to do the next day. These daily habits helped me settle my mind and brought our family closer together.

Science backs it up. Research shows that when parents engage intentionally, it leads to happier and more successful teens.[1] Parenting isn't about perfection. It's about being genuinely present, connecting deeply, and moving forward with purpose. Life's journey is full of difficulties, but it's these experiences that shape us.

It's common for us to doubt our abilities, wondering if we're doing a respectable job. But deep down, everyone has the potential to be an amazing parent.

In our journey to connect deeper with ourselves, paying attention to our inner voice is like tuning into the most real part of who we are. This inner essence is our true self, the part that stays constant even when we peel away all the layers of what everyone else thinks we should be. It's where our deepest wishes, beliefs, and goals live. Listening softly to this inner voice really means hearing what our heart and soul are trying to tell us, finding the quiet whispers of our own truth.

On this Inner Connection Quest, being available to listen to our inner being is key. It's about turning down the noise of the world and our busy thoughts to hear the wisdom that's always inside us. This wisdom might come to us as feelings, a gut instinct, or sudden clear thoughts that guide us to what feels right. By getting better at listening softly to this inner voice, we not only get to know ourselves on a deeper level but also gain the courage to be our most authentic selves.

By embracing our parenting journey with open hearts and minds, we discover our inner strength and confidence, especially when we're fully engaged and connected with our teens.

Flexibility: The Parenting Dance

Managing the parenting journey is like mastering a new skill or hobby. It thrives on consistent practice and patience, particularly when faced with unexpected challenges. Doubts may occasionally creep in. They're fueled by the tales we replay in our minds, like the moments when we fell short or wished for a second chance. However, these stories are not fixed. They progress as we gain fresh insights. This enables us to improve our parenting.

Consider the role of a parent to be like that of a sports coach. They guide teens from their current state, where they are stuck, to a future where they can be free to do what they want to do. Like coaching, parenting involves illuminating the path forward, helping teens see beyond immediate obstacles, fostering their growth, and empowering them with the confidence to trust in their abilities.

Parenting teens can also be compared to navigating a ship with the assistance of a tugboat. In this analogy, parents are the tugboat, providing guidance and direction to the huge vessel (the teens) to ensure it safely departs the harbor and reaches the open sea. Despite the ship's inherent strength and capability, the guidance of the tugboat is indispensable in maneuvering through the waters. This metaphor serves as a reminder of the impactful role parents play in supporting teens as they journey toward independence.

In a certification course called "Innate Wellbeing Specialist,"[2] I was introduced to a concept named FROGS, which I have since adapted to work for parenting. Reflect on the timeless fairy tale where a frog is transformed into royalty with a kiss. This narrative shows the transformative power of parenting, revealing the opportunities that unfold through this journey.

We don't need to be perfect parents or have perfect teens. Trying to be perfect makes everyone stressed. Parenting is about building a strong, loving bond, creating a place where everyone can grow and understand each other better without worrying about being perfect.

Let's start with 'Flexibility,' the "F" in the FROGS acronym. Being a flexible parent means you're able to adapt to new situations and problems that happen with teens without giving up your core beliefs and what's most important to you. The ability to be flexible is valuable in dealing with all the difficulties.

Talking to teens is like dancing. You both adjust to how the other moves. An example of this might be starting a conversation about grades. You can almost feel the air tighten, a bit like stepping on each other's toes. But then, you notice your teen's shoulders slump, a silent cue that they're not exactly enjoying the topic. So, you smoothly transition, softening your voice, maybe even cracking a light joke or sharing a comforting word. This shift is like finding the perfect tempo, showing you're not just stuck in one dance move.

This dance is much like the dance of conversation. You're not just sticking to your moves. You're paying attention to your partner, ready to adapt. When the mood lightens, you find that sweet spot where your teen opens up, sharing more than just a report card. They share their hopes, their worries, and maybe even a laugh with you. This dance becomes more than just steps. It's a bridge of understanding, connecting you two in a delicate but profound way.

Being flexible and willing to adapt to change when needed keeps our relationships with teens harmonious. In the coming chapters, we'll explore the FROGS framework more. Each letter in the acronym offers insights into becoming a better parent.

Parenting With Heart

Parenting with heart involves supporting and guiding our kids, starting with two big questions: "What do I want most for my family?" and "How can we make these wishes come true?" This journey is about more than just hoping for the best. It's about being there for our teens and turning challenges into chances to learn something valuable.

Our dedication to our values, as well as looking at problems in a new way, not only helps us grow but also teaches teens important lessons. They learn about sticking to it, thinking creatively to solve problems, and the value of stepping back to listen and let the noisy thoughts settle, especially when facing new challenges or fears.

For example, when I started making videos, I was really nervous about it. Stepping into the world of public speaking was like standing at the edge of a high dive for me, staring down into the unknown. It was sheer terror. But as I took this leap, I learned something not only about conquering fear but also about the act of letting go. Letting go of the heavy chains of past hesitations, of the stinging criticisms that once echoed in my mind. It was in this release that I found a new space to grow, a clearer path to refine and sharpen my speaking abilities.

With every talk I shared, I noticed progress in my communication. Each practice session didn't just inch me closer to becoming the communicator I dreamed of being. It was reshaping me into a more confident, more authentic version of myself. I wasn't just learning to speak better; I was learning to live more fully as me.

This journey from fear to freedom showed me that the ability to share one's ideas with confidence and clarity is within reach for anyone willing to step up to the challenge. It's not about being born a great speaker. It's about the willingness to grow, to embrace each opportunity to speak as a chance to improve and to express oneself more completely.

The shift happened when I let go of my fears. It unlocked a part of myself that I had kept hidden. The breakthrough came by thinking about how we are born with an innate ability to talk. I discovered the power that came from deep within myself. I realized that our voices are not just tools for communication but expressions of our unique identities and perspectives.

The way we see things can change our reality and can make a significant difference in how we parent and see the world. It can turn obstacles into chances to grow and get better. By opening up our minds, we can oversee tough situations more gracefully and experience more joy in life.

Realizing we can change our mindset is powerful. It shows us our view of things isn't set in stone. By clearing our minds, we see that we can overcome challenges. Stress often comes from comparing ourselves too much or setting goals too high.

Adopting a growth mindset regarding parenting means being okay with not knowing everything and leading with love. It's about being open to new things, being patient, and understanding that love grows over time. By doing this, we make our own lives better and create a supportive environment for teens to thrive.

Seeing challenges as chances to grow rather than setbacks invite us to view tough times as a level to beat in a shared adventure. How can we show teens that problems can be opportunities? Understanding feedback as a way to get better, not something to fear, can change how teens see critiques. How can we create a space where feedback is seen as helpful?

This chapter was about how important it is to connect with and understand teens as they figure out what they love. We learned that being a good parent means being able to change when needed and listening softly to what teens are going through. This can make challenging times opportunities to gain experience. We share this journey with our kids, helping them open their hearts and giving them all the love and support we can as they make their own way in the world.

Next, we're moving on to a story called "From Baby Girl to CEO." We'll see how the lessons of love and caring learned at home can have an influence on other areas of our lives. So, get ready for a story about how love can help us succeed and make the world a better place.

FROM BABY GIRL TO CEO

Love is more than just a feeling. It's a space that grows and includes all kinds of relationships: between parents and kids, brothers and sisters, and partners. There are distinct types of love, each with its own lessons and beauty.

From learning to share and having a good relationship with siblings to building a life with a spouse based on trust and teamwork, every experience teaches us more about love. Becoming a parent can open up a deeper, limitless, and unconditional love.

These dimensions of love aren't just steps we take one after the other. They're like rivers coming together, always moving and making our awareness of love richer. Genuine love is what keeps everything flourishing. It's a journey that begins when we're little and keeps flowing, changing, and growing with us.

Child's Dimension of Heart

When Emily was born, her family's world turned into an exciting adventure book. Her parents, Chelsea and Eric, were thrilled, ready for the fun journey of watching her grow and explore life. From her first day, Emily was surrounded by love and care, making every moment special.

As Emily grew, her parents were always there cheering her on. They answered all her curious questions and made sure her life was full of adventures, from exciting zoo visits to quiet times in the park. As Emily started showing her unique personality, her parents celebrated her achievements, helped her when things got tough, and taught her to be true to herself and caring to others.

Starting preschool was a milestone for Emily, bringing more independence and sometimes disagreements with her parents. But they knew this was all part of growing up. They gave her space to learn important lessons on her own while still guiding her gently.

Preschool sparked new interests for Emily, like art, music, and stories, helping her express herself in new ways. This time brought her even closer to her parents. Chelsea became the queen of bedtime stories, making every night magical with tales. Eric took Emily on nature adventures, teaching her about the beauty of the world around them.

Together, they made every day an exciting chapter in Emily's story, filled with love, fun, and discovery, showing just how wonderful growing up can be.

Emily's understanding of love and family was deeply rooted in the annual family camping trips, an experience that was more than just a tradition. It was a canvas where her worldview was painted in vivid colors of togetherness and resilience. One particular evening, as the campfire crackled with a comforting rhythm, casting dancing shadows around the circle of her family, Emily sat nestled between her parents. The air was filled with the rich scent of pine and the smoky aroma of the firewood, blending seamlessly with the occasional whiff of marshmallows roasting over the flames.

"Remember, Em, the world is much like this fire," her dad said softly, poking at the embers with a stick, sending a cascade of sparks into the night sky. "It can be unpredictable and sometimes harsh, but with warmth and light, we can make it beautiful."

Her mom added, laughing gently as she wrapped an arm around Emily, "And just like these marshmallows, life has its sweet moments, but if we're not careful, it can also get a bit sticky."

These moments, filled with the soothing sounds of the forest, the comforting warmth of the fire, and the laughter of her loved ones, were etched into Emily's memory. It was during these times that she learned the importance of warmth, resilience, and the beauty of life's simple joys.

Sibling's Dimension of Heart

Back when Chelsey was only three, Eric and Chelsea brought baby Jack home; the whole family buzzed with excitement, especially Emily, now a big sister. Though thrilled, Emily was a bit worried about sharing her parents' attention. To smooth things out, Eric and Chelsea made sure to spend special time with Emily, balancing her needs with Jack's.

As Jack grew, Emily stepped into her big sister's shoes with pride. She was there teaching Jack to crawl, sharing bedtime stories, and playing together. Jack's admiration made Emily feel more confident and responsible.

Their parents cheered on Emily's caring role, ensuring she knew how much they appreciated her. But, like all siblings, Emily and Jack had their squabbles over toys or who got more attention. These moments turned into lessons from Eric and Chelsea on how to solve disagreements and work as a team.

As teens, Emily and Jack found their own paths: Emily with her music and Jack with sports. Their parents were their biggest fans, cheering at Emily's concerts and Jack's games.

Despite the difficulties of teenage life, Emily and Jack stayed close, supporting each other through tough times, like friendship issues or school struggles.

Sure, there were times Emily felt a bit jealous of Jack being the youngest, and Jack sometimes felt overshadowed by Emily's successes. These feelings led to arguments, but their parents were always there to guide them through, teaching them to respect and listen to each other.

Through it all, Emily and Jack's bond grew stronger, evolving into a deep friendship that would last a lifetime.

———

Helping siblings like Emily and Jack forge a strong, loving bond is a vital part of parenting. This connection is crucial for their emotional growth, especially as they navigate the complexities of teenage social circles. Guiding them to treat friends with the same care as siblings lays the foundation for friendships rooted in respect, empathy, and understanding.

Sibling dynamics teaches teens about deep connections and sets the stage for future relationships, emphasizing loyalty and real connection. It's a practice ground for building meaningful friendships.

Encouraging good friendship skills leads teens to form stronger, lasting bonds. They learn to value friends who respect them and share their interests and values, enriching their lives. This approach fosters supportive, growth-oriented friendships, far beyond mere romantic interests, creating a network of relationships that are enriching and supportive.

———

As years passed, their family camping trips evolved. The conversations shifted from tales of folklore and family anecdotes to deeper discussions about love and life.

One night, under a tapestry of stars, Emily ventured to ask, "How do you know if you're making the right choices in life?"

Her parents exchanged a knowing glance before her dad replied, "You may not always know right away, Em. Sometimes, it's about taking the best step forward you can, with love and consideration as your compass."

Her mom squeezed her hand, adding, "And remember, making mistakes is part of the journey. It's how we learn, grow, and find our way back to what truly matters."

Jack, with energy to spare, would often chime in with his own youthful insights, "It's like when you're on the field, and you have to decide in a split second whether to pass or shoot," he'd say with earnestness, eager to contribute to the conversation. His sports analogies, while out of left field, reminded them all that wisdom can come from unexpected sources.

These dialogues, rich with wisdom and humor, shaped Emily's understanding of the world around her. They taught her that life was a mosaic of experiences, each one a step toward understanding deeper truths about love, family, and the essence of human connection.

Spouse's Dimension of Heart

Chelsea and Eric's journey together as a couple turned out to be more complex than Chelsea first thought. Initially, their relationship felt as easy as floating down a river, hand in hand, lost in love. But as time went on, challenges like money worries and the busy life of raising kids put their love to the test, making their bond even stronger in the end. Their challenging work made the commitment to each other solid and their relationship tougher.

Finding the right balance between their individual wishes and their life together was a pivotal lesson. They learned the importance of not letting personal desires overshadow their marriage's needs, where compromise and teamwork are vital. Open discussions about their hopes and compromises helped strengthen their connection.

They realized that maintaining a fulfilling relationship requires constant work, care, and dedication. By sharing their spiritual journey, staying emotionally connected, and being role models for Emily and Jack, they discovered that love is a commitment to grow together and make their marriage thrive.

———

Marriage symbolizes the joining of two lives, yet it's essential to acknowledge the variety of family dynamics that exist. Some parents may be on solo journeys or navigating co-parenting arrangements after separation. The significant part, across these different scenarios, is fostering an environment where love, respect, and empathy flourish. These core values nurture strong, healthy relationships.

For parents going through transitions, such as single parenthood or after a marriage ends, maintaining a consistent presence of love and demonstrating resilience are essential. This steadfastness offers teens a firsthand lesson in adapting to life's changes with grace and strength.

The aim is to internalize and then model behaviors rooted in respect, empathy, and compassion, regardless of marital status or spiritual affiliation. This inward focus on cultivating personal virtues guides teens in understanding meaningful relationships. It emphasizes that the foundation of any strong relationship lies within us, shaped by our actions and attitudes, and is independent of external circumstances. This lesson equips teens with the insight to build their own futures on the principles of love and mutual respect, reflecting the inner growth and strength they've observed at home.

Parent's Dimension of Heart

Chelsea and Eric quickly learned that being parents meant diving all in. The moment Emily arrived, they knew they had to show her all the love, understanding, and selflessness they could muster.

When Emily became a big sister to little Jack, it was clear to Chelsea and Eric that their job as parents was to keep their focus sharp. They aimed to create a loving and safe home, teach good behavior, and always be there for Emily and Jack.

Their strong marriage was the foundation of their family life, showing them how important it is to have a loving and giving relationship for being great parents. They naturally became more giving, patient, and forgiving.

Despite the hurdles, parenting was the most rewarding journey for them. Watching Emily and Jack grow and thrive filled them with immense joy and pride.

Chelsea and Eric saw their distinct roles in parenting as strengths. They brought their own styles and experiences to the table, making a rich and balanced world for Emily and Jack.

Chelsea was the comforting heart of the home, always there to listen, comfort, and support. She ensured the house was a place of peace and understanding, where Emily and Jack felt safe and loved. She often sat down with them to discuss their day and feelings, helping them grow confident and emotionally stable.

On the other hand, Eric was all about bringing adventure into their lives. He organized family outings and activities that strengthened their bonds. He took Emily and Jack on nature hikes, museum visits, and sports, sparking their curiosity and teaching them about teamwork and the joy of exploring.

Together, Chelsea and Eric's parenting styles balanced each other. Chelsea provided a safe, comforting base, while Eric encouraged exploration and learning. This combination helped Emily and Jack become well-rounded, understanding the depth of love and ready to take on the world.

Their endearing love for each other and unwavering commitment to their family was their driving force. Chelsea and Eric knew parenting was a long-term commitment, a journey they were more than willing to embark on for the sake of their children's futures.

Evolution of Love

The happiness that comes with being a parent is made up of many moments, from the simple joy of hearing your child laugh to the great pride you feel in their accomplishments. The most rewarding part is watching the bond between parent and child grow and deepen, lifting the whole parenting journey to new levels of joy.

Stepping into the role of a grandparent can open up a whole new world of delight. Grandparents can become wise old trees, offering shade and advice through all of life's difficulties. Their experience gives them a unique viewpoint that can provide priceless wisdom, making a significant difference in their grandchildren's lives.

Family life takes us on a path through distinct roles, from being a child to a sibling, then a spouse, and finally a parent. Each role offers lessons in love, emotional growth, and moral understanding. Shifting from self-centeredness to a deeper care for others expands our capacity to love. Our ultimate aim? To cultivate a heart brimming with selfless love, becoming a beacon of inspiration for the next generation.

Just as we strive for emotional growth and a spirit of giving within our families, these principles can profoundly transform any environment we encounter. Bringing altruistic love into our interactions, whether at work or in the community, can significantly enhance our well-being and that of those around us. For instance, practicing empathy when others face challenges, offering support during community projects, or extending patience to those learning new skills can cultivate a culture of kindness and cooperation. These acts of compassion and understanding can spread to any situation, turning daily interactions into chances for positive change and strengthening our connections everywhere we go.

Reviving the Workplace

A dedicated employee named James had been working in his dream job for years, but things recently started feeling a bit off. The company faced tough times, with many layoffs, causing some of his close friends at work to leave. This situation made the workplace feel gloomy and made James wonder if he should look for a new job.

Then, Emily became the new CEO. She was known for turning companies around and bringing fresh energy to the team. Emily believed the key to success was ensuring the employees were happy and doing well.

One of the first things Emily did was to sit down and listen to what everyone had to say about their jobs. She wanted to know what the employees liked and what they thought could be better. To do this, she held meetings where people could speak freely and also sent out surveys to get everyone's input.

She found out that people wanted two main things: to have more control over their work hours and to get more chances to learn new skills. So, Emily made some changes. She let people choose when they worked as long as the work got done. This meant they could drop off their kids at school or go to a doctor's appointment without stress. She also set up training sessions where people could learn new things related to their jobs, which made them feel more excited and confident about their work.

These changes made a significant difference. With flexible hours, employees felt happier because they could manage their time better, fitting work around their lives instead of the other way around. The training sessions helped them improve at their jobs and aim for higher positions within the company. Overall, Emily's changes made the workplace a much happier and more satisfying place to be, and it helped the company do better, too.

James noticed these changes and felt a renewed sense of enthusiasm for his job. People started working together more effectively and felt a stronger connection to what the company was trying to achieve.

Thanks to Emily's leadership, the company began to do well financially, which successfully allowed them to upgrade their technology and equipment. But, for James, the best part was seeing the workplace transform into a happy and satisfying place to be. Emily's approach and her commitment to the team had turned the company into a wonderful place to work again.

———

In every family, there's a really important lesson about finding the right mix between what we want for ourselves and what's best for everyone. It's all about balancing our own freedom with staying close and strong as a family. This balance helps us all get along better, not just at home but with others, too.

Studies have shown that when families are strong and supportive, kids feel better about themselves, do better in school, and learn right from wrong.[1] It's at home that we first learn how to think about what others need, not just what we want. This is super important for having a good relationship with people and feeling happy.

When we show kindness and understanding, we make our home a place where everyone feels supported. This is what happened with Emily. Growing up in a caring family, she learned to see the world in a way that's full of compassion, which made it natural for her to connect with others and make a positive difference in her community.

Emily's parents, Chelsea and Eric, taught her all about love and looking out for others. By sharing these values, they achieved their goal of raising someone who really wants to make the world a better place. This shows how powerful it can be when we start making positive changes at home.

Building Rapport

The 'R' in FROGS stands for 'Rapport,' which is really important between parents and teens. Rapport means understanding someone, understanding their world, and appreciating what makes them special. This connection is vital to having a good relationship with your kids, especially during the teen years.

Think about how Emily made her workplace better by going out of her way to listen to what her employees needed and make them feel valued. Parents can do something similar with their teens. It's not about using fancy tricks. It's about creating a natural bond.

Creating rapport is more than just talking. It's about listening softly and connecting on a deeper level. It's hearing the emotions behind the words, making a safe space where teens can be themselves without fear of being judged. Parents can aim to see things from their teen's viewpoint, offering a shoulder to lean on, not just quick fixes.

This isn't about dismissing their problems. It's about being someone teens trust, who can face challenges with them and help find peace together. It's in these moments when we listen and understand that we build a strong, trusting relationship.

Being present for teens is crucial for building rapport. In today's fast-paced world, dedicating undivided attention to someone can be incredibly meaningful. It's about spending quality time together, whether that involves discussing life's big questions, enjoying fun activities, or simply relaxing without any distractions.

For instance, after picking Emily up from school, Chelsea noticed her usually chatty daughter was silent. Her brows furrowed in a mix of frustration and sadness. As they drove home, Chelsea saw an opportunity to reinforce their bond. Aware of the importance of maintaining a strong rapport, especially during these moments, she initiated a gentle conversation.

"Sweetie, you seem a bit down today. Want to talk about it?" Chelsea asked, her voice soft and inviting.

Emily sighed, "It's just...Sophie. She didn't invite me to her birthday party. I thought we were friends."

Chelsea parked the car and turned to face Emily, ensuring she had her full attention—a crucial step in building rapport. "That sounds really tough, honey. I remember a time when I felt left out, too. It hurts, doesn't it?"

Emily nodded, her eyes meeting her mom's, feeling genuine concern and empathy.

Chelsea continued, "Sometimes, people make choices that can hurt us, but it doesn't always mean they intended to. There's a reason Sophie couldn't invite you. Have you had a chance to talk to her about it?"

"No... I just assumed she didn't want me there," Emily admitted, her voice small.

Chelsea gently suggested, "Maybe you could ask her about it? It might help clear things up. Remember, understanding others starts with a conversation. You're great at making friends and talking to people. I believe in you, Em."

Emily considered her mom's words, feeling the warmth of her support. "I guess I could try talking to Sophie tomorrow. Thanks."

Chelsea smiled, "Anytime, love you, sweetie."

This conversation was a turning point for Emily. Chelsea's approach of listening strengthened their relationship and taught Emily a crucial life skill.

Emily's story, from her family's loving home to becoming a CEO who changed her company for the better, shows the amazing impact of empathy and understanding. These skills were crucial to her success, showing the power of family values in personal and professional life.

The Inner Connection Quest enhances our family ties through soft listening, empathetic understanding, and compassionate actions. It invites us to be consistently caring and considerate. True love for our family extends beyond mere presence. It involves tapping into our inner strength and actively seeking ways to strengthen and celebrate our connections.

This chapter demonstrates how familial support can inspire us to achieve remarkable feats. For instance, it details how James regained his motivation at work with encouragement from Emily. The Inner Connection Quest emphasizes the importance of listening attentively and supporting one another to ensure every family member feels heard and valued.

After taking time to absorb this chapter, get ready to start a new chapter called "Striking the Right Chords." Imagine believing in yourself so much that it lifts you from just dreaming as a kid to doing amazing things when you grow up. We'll see how being loved and believed in can do more than help one teen. It can spread out and have an influence on many people.

Next up, we'll get to know the TRUE LOVE qualities that can make teens stand out. This next chapter can help us think, in new ways, about having dreams and the whole adventure of life. So, come along as we imagine a world where young people glow with love and a belief in their inner value.

STRIKING THE RIGHT CHORDS

Growing up, my mom was like a cheerleader, lifting me up because she knew I had amazing potential. She had an encouraging way of saying things like, "You might marry a prince, so why don't you start behaving like you live in a castle." It sounded like something out of a storybook, but her real message was that she believed in me. It was the wind beneath my wings.

As a parent, I tried to sprinkle that same kind of magic dust of optimism and solid backing into my kids' lives. Pulling from my own upbringing, I've crafted a set of qualities that I think make up an impressive teen. I like to call these qualities TRUE LOVE, a catchy way to remember some really important traits that can help them shine.

Seeing parenting through this lens turns it into an adventure. Challenges we face together make our family ties stronger, like the epic journeys' heroes go on in stories, where each test brings them closer to wisdom and strength. Being a parent is like being on a quest filled with scary yet enlightening moments that teach us how to bond more deeply and grow right alongside our kids.

Just imagine a future where your teens have grown up, starting families of their own, and you're looking back at the journey of their growth. Think about how rewarding it would feel to see them living out those core values you've helped instill in them.

But let's keep it real. The path isn't always going to be smooth. Teens won't always reflect these values perfectly in everything they do. Each kid is on their own unique path, which means we can adapt these ideals to fit them and our family's unique shape. The real win isn't about sticking rigidly to a list of values but about nurturing a vision that lifts and guides us all. When teens feel loved and believe in their endless potential, there's no telling how far they'll go.

Let's pause to consider the concept of "being versus doing." When we focus on staying true to ourselves, our original nature can guide us toward the right resources, like a book or a training that resonates deeply. Being conscious of our magnificence allows us to express our inner selves. This awareness leads us to feel optimistic about who we are, eliminating judgment or feelings of inadequacy. There's no necessity for pretense or obsessing over results.

Adopting this perspective, we can face the future with open hearts and minds. Envision the myriad of possibilities that can emerge when we, along with our teens, navigate life guided by the intrinsic values we hold dear, propelled by the essence of our true selves.

This journey of becoming our true selves, that unique self that can only be expressed by us, underscores the idea that we all possess remarkable characteristics waiting to be revealed. In doing so, our society can transform into a melting pot of these splendid traits, enriching our collective experience with the diversity and depth of who we truly are.

So, let's dive into imagining all the bright futures that could unfold, powered by the Inner Connection Quest, where we are one with our inner strengths.

T - Trustworthy Actions

Imagine teens who not only promise to help out more but also surprise everyone by turning the messy garage into a neat space, all on their own. These teens find things everyone thought were lost and recycle stuff that's no longer needed. Their actions, from the little promises to the big surprises, prove that being trustworthy is about doing what you say you'll do.

R - Refined Character

Picture teens who make a new student feel welcome by inviting them to lunch and introducing them to friends. These teens don't stop there. They share their own school experiences, making the new students laugh and feel at home. This shows teens know the value of making someone feel included, which is a part of having a good character.

U - Upstanding Citizen

Envision teens who love nature and not only join local clean-up events but also start a recycling project at school. They teach others how to recycle properly and why it's important, showing they care deeply about the environment. These teens' actions inspire others to take care of the planet, too, showing they understand their role in making the world a better place.

E - Excellence Attitude

Consider teens who see group projects as chances to work well with others, ensuring everyone's ideas are heard. They prefer teamwork over winning alone, believing that success comes from everyone doing well together. These teen volunteers help those in need, showing they know the real win is in making a positive difference in others' lives.

L - Loyal Heart

Consider teens who value their friends deeply, even amidst their busy lives. They support their friends and family through both good times and bad, showing that true loyalty involves meaningful engagement and consistent support. These teens understand the importance of standing by others and how loyalty strengthens every relationship.

O - Open for Growth

Visualize teens as individuals eager to learn and grow, viewing challenges as opportunities for development. Their readiness to embrace new experiences significantly enriches their personal growth. They regularly seek feedback on their actions and decisions, embracing it as a crucial tool to continually improve, adapt, and evolve in their journey.

V - Visionary Outlook

Imagine teens who jump at the chance to try new things. They approach situations with a sense of curiosity and the belief that every hurdle is an opportunity to innovate and redefine what's possible. Their enthusiasm for exploring uncharted territories not only broadens their horizons but also inspires those around them to think creatively and ambitiously.

E - Effective Connections

What about teens who excel in rallying support for their vision, connecting with community members and inspiring action? These teens understand that realizing big dreams requires not just personal effort but also cultivating strong partnerships. By fostering connections and sharing their enthusiasm, they help others see the potential for positive change together.

———

Loving teens right now, just as they are, is vital while we cheer them on to grow into their best selves. It's not about waiting for them to be perfect. We're with them every step of the way, chatting, laughing, and showing them they can do remarkable things. Every day is about giving them a boost, believing in them, and showing lots of love.

But what happens if our teens start wandering off the path we hoped for? First off, we need to clear our heads of all those worries about teens getting into trouble. We should trust that our teens have this incredible inner strength and wisdom to make things right. When it's time to offer some guidance, it's all about asking them first, "Hey, do you want to hear my thoughts on this?" This way, we make sure we're coming from a place of positivity, not loaded down with worries or doubts.

For example, let's say a teen is spending too much time on video games and their grades start slipping. Instead of jumping straight into lecture mode, a parent might say, "I've noticed you're really into your games lately, which is cool, but how do you feel about your latest report card?" This opens up a conversation, making space for the teen to think and ask for advice on balancing fun and responsibilities.

Our goal isn't just to prepare them for someday. It's about appreciating who they are right now, in this moment. Teen life is tough, with school stress and trying to fit in. That's why we keep the conversation going, listen respectfully, and remind each family member how much they're valued.

When teens mess up or stray, it's not just a hiccup. It's a learning moment. Staying positive and keeping those heart-to-heart talks going can turn a mistake into a stepping stone. For instance, if a teen comes home past curfew, instead of getting mad right away, a parent might say, "Let's talk about last night. I was worried, but I also know we can figure out a better plan together." This shows trust and opens up a dialogue for setting boundaries and understanding consequences.

Creating this kind of home, where teens know they're loved and respected, gives them the courage to face challenges head-on and discover more about themselves. We're not just guiding them through the teenage years. We're equipping them to navigate life with a smile, knowing they have the wisdom inside them to become who they are meant to be and that they've got a robust support system in their corner.

Tuning Into Our Family Symphony

Think of our family as a unique band, with each person adding their own sound to our group tune. Laughs, arguments, and quiet moments all add up to our family's special music.

But, let's be honest, it can be challenging. Teens deal with a lot, like figuring out social media, school stress, and finding out who they are. These challenges can make our family tune a bit off at times.

Parenting teens is like being a band leader during a tricky song. We face disagreements and demands for independence, but we always find a way back to a smooth tune.

It's not about being perfect but about embracing the off notes, learning from them, and making our family stronger. By listening and adjusting to each other, we create a real, touching tune, even with its flaws.

Talking openly with teens, especially when things are tough, can change our family dynamic. It's more than making rules; it's about conversations that help them deal with challenges and see their strengths.

We want to build a family where openness, kindness, and growing together are essential. In our family band, everyone's part is essential, making sure each voice is valued, adding to our song's harmony.

We're creating a family melody that shows the best of us, fitting together perfectly. It's about making a space where everyone can be themselves and still fit in. Through difficulties, we're making something special. We're a family that sticks together, supports each other, and has fun, especially through the teen years, with lots of laughter and love.

Shaping Outcomes

Leaping into 'Outcome' in our FROGS strategy, we're focusing on guiding our teens through the exciting journey of discovering their passions and aspirations. This step is all about blending our hopes for them with their own visions for the future.

Talking about 'Outcome' means having relaxed, open conversations that explore teens' dreams and goals. It's all on the table, from career paths they're curious about to the personal qualities they aim to embody.

To spark these conversations, we can start by exploring the qualities they admire in others and wish to embody. Asking, "Who do you look up to for their courage?" or "In your opinion, what qualities define a good person?" serves as more than conversation starters for teens. These questions encourage reflection about their own aspirations and values.

To keep these dialogues engaging, we can weave them into the fabric of their daily experiences and the wider world. Highlighting how these admired traits manifest in real-life scenarios makes the concept of personal growth not just intriguing but also connected to their reality. This approach keeps the journey of maturing both exciting and relevant to them.

Helping teens on this self-discovery trip means being part of their learning journey. Volunteer together or find books and movies that spark new interests. It's all about giving them chances to ask questions, learn, and figure out their place in the world.

For instance, if teens admire someone's ability to lead, we can talk about what makes a good leader and then brainstorm ways they can practice leadership, like leading a team project or joining a club.

To maintain the momentum of these conversations, we can celebrate their triumphs, reflect on their growth, and set new objectives together. This mix of encouragement and attentive listening adapts as their interests evolve and their sense of self transforms.

Let's give teens a safe space to express their thoughts and emotions without fear of judgment. This sense of security encourages them to be more open and communicative.

As teens' perspectives and values shift, it's helpful to be flexible. Demonstrating our respect for their growing independence and self-perception keeps the lines of communication open and dynamic.

Connecting with teens means being interested in what's on their minds and in their hearts. Embracing a style of listening softly is being there for them in a caring and patient way. This means having meaningful chats, exchanging thoughts, and acknowledging their feelings with an open attitude. This journey isn't about shaping them to fit our idea of who they should become. It's about backing them up as they discover and accept their authentic selves. By practicing this gentle way of listening, we encourage them to open up more fully and genuinely.

Riding the Waves

Parent: I've noticed you've seemed a bit down lately. Want to talk about what's on your mind?

Teen: Yeah, it's just... I always feel like I'm not doing enough. It just feels like I'm always messing up or not doing as well as my friends.

Parent: It sounds like you're putting a lot of pressure on yourself. Remember, it's not about doing everything perfectly. Life's more about finding out who you really want to be.

Teen: But isn't aiming for the best important? I just don't want to disappoint you or anyone.

Parent: Aiming for the best is good, but understanding what's really important is what matters. It's okay to make mistakes. That's how we learn and grow.

Teen: I guess I'm scared of making mistakes.

Parent: Everyone makes mistakes, and that's perfectly okay. It's not the mistakes that define us but how we respond to them. Bringing your worries into the open, like now, helps a lot.

Teen: But what if my mistakes are too big?

Parent: What you see as flaws or mistakes doesn't determine your worth. Think of them as feedback, not as something that defines you. It's a chance for you to learn and for your true self to shine through.

Teen: So, I should just accept when I mess up?

Parent: Accepting doesn't mean being okay with not trying. It means not letting fear of failure stop you from growing. It's about learning from your experience and moving forward.

Teen: That makes sense. I just wish it didn't feel so tough.

Parent: It's normal to feel that way. But remember, I'm here for you.

Teen: Thanks, I really needed to hear that.

Parent: Anytime. And remember, there's no one in the world quite like you. I'm proud of you, not only for what you achieve, but for who you are.

———

Through open conversations, as illustrated in the dialogue between Parent and Teen, we can see that our perceived flaws and the critical thoughts that sometimes overwhelm us should be viewed as opportunities for growth. Our errors don't determine our worth.

Approaching teens without preconceived notions and believing in their limitless potential is crucial for their development and our own. It's about mutual discovery, support, and guiding with an open heart.

Just like a garden that thrives with sunlight, water, and care, the journey of growth and development for both parents and teens is a process that requires patience, understanding, and nurturing. Imagine the human spirit as a garden. Sometimes, weeds of doubt and clouds of uncertainty may obscure the beauty and potential within. Yet, it's through the diligent gardening of our thoughts and emotions, pulling out those weeds and trusting in the sun's return, that we discover the resilience and joy that lie waiting beneath the surface.

No matter what tough times we go through or how messy things get, we're still valuable and strong deep down. This toughness is like finding a $20 bill that's dirty, wrinkled, and a bit torn. At first, it might not look as nice as a brand-new bill. But it's worth just as much when you use it to buy something. This tells us a lot about our own lives. Life can be rough, making us feel worn out. Sometimes, we might think we're not as good because of the tough times we've been through. Just like that tough $20 bill, we're still just as valuable.

Our innate light shines bright, no matter how often life has knocked us around. Understanding our true worth and bringing out our inner light can help us find the happiness and simplicity we thought were gone. This isn't about dealing with what's outside. It's about seeing and loving the bright spirit we all have inside.

Parents possess the inner resilience to overcome challenges, serving as beacons of strength and support for their teens. By listening attentively, encouraging open communication, and fostering an environment of unconditional understanding, we not only navigate tough times but also inspire teens to develop their best selves with confidence and perseverance.

Popping Doubts, Finding Hope

As the winter evening wrapped the world outside in a blanket of twilight and soft rain, I found myself cozy in my favorite chair, lost in thought. My mind wandered back to the summer day of my grandchild's birthday party, where a simple bubble machine, once just a source of fun, took on a new, meaningful role in my reflections.

Watching the kids chase and pop bubbles, laughing each time one burst, I realized something important. What if I treated my negative thoughts the same way? I acknowledge them but don't let them control my feelings? This idea was a game changer. Suddenly, every negative thought was just a temporary bubble, within my power to pop and let go of before it could bring me down.

This new way of thinking helped me see my worries and doubts as bubbles. When I caught myself feeling down or defeated, I imagined popping these thought bubbles, letting them disappear. This mental exercise of releasing negativity brought me a lightness and freedom I hadn't felt in a long time. It was as though with every popped bubble, I was letting go of a bit of darkness and letting in more light.

This approach isn't just for dealing with personal doubts. It can also help us see worries in a new light. Parenting a teen is full of moments that might feel like bubbles of challenge and emotion. But what if we could pop the bubbles of anxiety and fear about our teens' futures, trusting in their ability to grow and find their way? Recognizing and then letting go of these worries can help us create a positive, hopeful environment for them to thrive in.

By seeing thoughts of challenges and successes as bubbles, we learn to let go of (pop) the small stuff and celebrate (catch) the good moments. This mindset encourages empathy, open talks, and a stronger bond between parents and teens. It shows teens how to face their challenges with a positive outlook, learning to pop their own bubbles of doubt and move forward with confidence.

This lesson from a child's birthday party was a powerful insight into life and parenting. It taught me that our thoughts can change.

Life can be full of hope, and joy is just a thought away. New thoughts become new changes. We can look for possibilities in the mind and opportunities in the world.

This chapter explores the power of hope and the resilience needed to persevere. Celebrating even the smallest victories can remind us that growth and learning are continuous processes. How can we celebrate these crucial but modest achievements in ways that help teens recognize the importance of their positive steps?

Through the Inner Connection Quest, we maintain our belief in teens, even when the path ahead seems uncertain. We know deep down that we possess the necessary strength, love, and wisdom to guide them through the complexities of adolescence. It's about employing a gentle approach, leveraging our inner reserves of patience, understanding, and support.

By creating a home where TRUE LOVE values, good talks, and celebrating each person's path are part of everyday life, we're setting the stage for teens to do well. It reminds us that in the journey of growing up is a beautiful story of evolving our hearts, finding out who we are, and loving each other without conditions.

As we conclude the chapter on guiding teens, we've discovered the power of supporting them in popping the bubbles of doubt and fear. We've seen that by building a home filled with hope, encouragement, and recognition of every small victory, we create a setting where teens feel valued and understood. This journey is about believing in their potential and showing them that, together, we have the strength to face any challenge.

After giving this chapter enough contemplation, move forward to "I Thought You Forgot About Me," where we hear Savannah's story. It brings to light some struggles and emotions of dealing with the teenage years. As we step into this next chapter, let's remember the lessons of love and the crucial role we play in the lives of the teens we care about.

"I THOUGHT YOU FORGOT ABOUT ME"

It was getting late when Savannah finished her shift at a small-town department store. The summer night was muggy as she stood outside the store, waiting. At sixteen, this job was her first attempt in the working world, and she found little to enjoy about it. Her mom was supposed to pick her up, but as she stood alone in the now-empty parking lot, it became clear that everyone else had left.

As the minutes turned into what felt like hours, Savannah's frustration grew. The thought that her mom might have forgotten her became a sinking feeling. Deciding not to wait any longer, she began her walk home, concealed in the darkness of the night.

The walk lasted about twenty minutes, a solitary trek that weighed heavily on her. The idea that parents should be a source of support and make their children feel valued felt like a stark contrast to her reality. To Savannah, this moment was another painful reminder of her belief that her parents didn't genuinely care about her, that she wasn't worthy of love.

Halfway through her walk, the glow of headlights appeared in the distance. As the vehicle drew closer, Savannah recognized it as her family's van. Overcome with bitterness, she concealed herself in the bushes, watching as the van passed by without stopping. She doubted her mom would have noticed her even if she hadn't hidden.

Upon reaching her house, Savannah's mom emerged, frantic and loud, questioning, "Where were you?!" The worry in her voice did little to mask the underlying tension. "I was so worried something happened."

I walked home," was Savannah's quiet response.

"Why would you do that?!"

I thought you forgot about me," Savannah explained, her voice low, embodying a patience she didn't feel. "I thought you didn't care about me."

The look of anger and hurt that crossed her mom's face was palpable. "Why would you say that?!" she yelled back. "I guess I'm just a horrible mother!"

With that, her mom turned and stormed back into the house, leaving Savannah alone in the dark. The silence echoed her feelings of abandonment. There was no hug, no words of comfort, only a stark confirmation of her deepest fears and emotions.

Savannah is a real person that I know. Her name was changed to protect her identity, but her story is true. She is an adult now with a family of her own.

I wanted to sit down with Savannah and discuss her journey to find her value. In the following conversation, she talks about how she was raised, how her parents affected her feelings of self-worth, and how she is healing from it now.

What was daily life like for you as a teen? Life was pretty lonely. I often had to fend for myself because my home environment was challenging. It seemed like I was always trying to sort things out on my own without much help from anyone. I had to be my own pillar of support. Everything at home felt uncertain, and I felt the need to be strong since I couldn't lean on my family for the support I needed.

My mom struggled to provide emotional support. She was usually overwhelmed with her own issues. My dad had a short temper, causing everyone in the house to be cautious around him to prevent any outbursts. I would often retreat into sleep or daydream about happier places. My bedroom became my safe haven where I could take a breath and find some peace.

What do you wish your parents did for you? I wished they had been more understanding and supportive. Whenever I made a mistake, instead of reacting with anger, I hoped they would reassure me, tell me it was okay, and show me love. I always felt pressured to meet their expectations. It left me feeling overly cautious and somewhat fearful of new situations.

I constantly found myself assessing my safety and wondering about the intentions of the people around me. I found myself bracing for something to go wrong. Allowing me to openly discuss my feelings without fear of a negative reaction or punishment would have made a significant difference. Knowing it was okay to express myself would have been incredibly freeing.

So, what is your personality? I'm quirky, fun, silly, and I like to joke and have a fun time. I'm more relaxed and chilled. I like get-togethers, and I'm a people person. I'm loud and crazy sometimes or super silly. Healing has helped me come out of my shell and be who I am and want to be. I'm freer to be me now instead of trying to fit into my parents' expectations.

From Shadows to Sunshine

Savannah's life was like a garden that didn't get enough sun, always stuck in the shade. The big shadows from her past, like feeling alone, not getting enough support, and family problems, kept her from seeing the light. But Savannah wanted to change this. She started to work on herself.

Changing her thoughts helped her see the difference between the bad memories of her past and the good things about her life now. She focused on what makes her strong, letting the story of her own growth lead the way.

This change was important for Savannah. It showed her that she didn't have to stay in the same environment she grew up in. By taking care of herself, she started doing better, finding out that her value didn't depend on others but on the light; she found it within herself.

With new thoughts, Savannah found a way to bring light and life to her world, much like nurturing a garden that had been in the shadows for too long. She discovered that feeling good about herself was something she had to work on regularly, just like caring for a garden.

This realization helped her feel strong and valuable on her own, no matter what her past was like. Her journey from tough times to finding her own light is a powerful example of how resilient and incredible people can be. It shows us that no matter what we've gone through, we can take care of ourselves, find our inner light, and shine in our own unique way.

Remote Controlling Our Feelings

Imagine we all have a special remote control. This isn't just any remote. It can change how we feel in a flash. Now, most of us think this remote is used by the people and things around us. If a friend says something, if the family does something, or if something unexpected happens, it's like they're pushing the buttons on our remote, making us feel happy, sad, or annoyed.

But guess what? We're actually the ones holding our remote. The way we think about what's happening to us really decides how we feel. Our minds are powerful. They can make real feelings just from our thoughts. So, if we choose to think about uplifting things, we can make ourselves feel better, no matter what's going on around us. It's like picking a comedy show to watch to cheer us up.

Realizing we have this power uplifts us. It means we can pick which thoughts to pay attention to and which to let go of. Picture a rainy day that makes everything look grey. But then, we decide to think about something exciting coming up, and suddenly, the day doesn't seem so grey anymore. We've changed the channel in our minds to something brighter.

Think of our feelings like a big box of crayons with all sorts of colors. Our thoughts are like our hands picking out which crayons to color with. Some days, we might choose calm blues and greens, and other days, bright yellows and oranges for happiness and excitement. We get to choose which colors to put on our day's canvas.

This ties back to how our thoughts shape our feelings, and those feelings fuel the energy and motivation that drive us from the inside. When we understand that our thoughts can influence our emotions, we realize the power we hold over our own internal landscape. Being in charge of our feelings doesn't mean we ignore the tough times. Instead, it's about leaning more into the good feelings, the ones that lift us up and bring us joy.

We have the choice to steer our thoughts in a direction that makes us feel better and more hopeful. By doing this, we're taking control of our inner dialogue, making conscious choices about what we focus on, and in turn, shaping our emotional well-being. We emerge stronger, more adaptable, and ready to face whatever comes next with a steady heart and a resilient spirit.

The point is, we're the ones using the remote, picking the channels of our emotions. It's a way to make every day brighter, knowing we have the power to choose how we feel. This is our secret power to living a happier life.

"Harvey" and the Lesson of Choosing Our Focus

The story of "Harvey," a movie from 1950, introduces us to a unique tale about Elwood P. Dowd and his unusual friend. Harvey isn't just any friend. He's a giant rabbit that only Elwood can see. This friendship brings up a lot of funny and profound moments in the movie, showing us how our beliefs shape how we see the world.

Elwood really believes in Harvey, even though Harvey isn't visible to anyone else. This part of the story helps us understand how we might sometimes hold onto thoughts that aren't based on what's real.

One scene that sticks out is when Elwood is at a social event, treating Harvey as if he's right there with him, even offering him a chair. This confuses everyone watching, but Elwood's actions show how real Harvey is to him despite Harvey being imaginary to everyone else.

For example, a teen is stressing out over a big test. They're convinced they're going to fail, even though they've studied and are well-prepared. This worry becomes their "Harvey," a giant, overwhelming rabbit of anxiety they can't seem to ignore.

Our first reaction might be to dive into that stress with them, echoing their fears and anxieties. But that's like feeding their "Harvey," making the rabbit grow even larger and more daunting in their mind.

Instead, acknowledging that this overwhelming emotion is their "Harvey," we can approach it differently. We can sit with them and say, "I see you're really worried about this test. Let's talk about what you've done to prepare." Through conversation, we guide them to recognize their hard work and preparation, helping them see that their fear of failing is much bigger in their mind than it should be. It's not dismissing their feelings but helping them to differentiate between the reality of their preparation and the imaginary scenario of failure they've built up.

This approach doesn't feed their "Harvey." It shrinks it back down to size by shifting focus from the fear of what might happen to the reality of their readiness and abilities. It's a way of showing them that, just like Elwood's belief in Harvey, sometimes our worries don't have a basis in our current reality. By not "feeding" into the exaggerated fears, we help our teens learn to manage their emotions more effectively, seeing challenges with clarity rather than through the lens of unnecessary worry.

"Harvey" teaches us not to focus too much on those imaginary thoughts that don't have a real base. The scenario could be about anything, such as responding to the actions of others, frustration of a situation, or an attitude toward someone. It shows us to be mindful of where we put our mental momentum, encouraging us to keep to thoughts that lift us up and let go of the ones that don't.

The Leaks and the Bucket

After hearing about "Harvey" and Elwood's special but invisible friend, we're inclined to think about our own Harveys. These are the worries or fears we make a big deal out of, even though they might not really be there. Just like Elwood with Harvey, we sometimes pay too much attention to these thoughts, giving them more room in our lives than they deserve. This story leads us to an idea about changing our habits and fixing the "leaks" in our lives.

Picture trying to stop a leak with just a bucket. It might catch the drips and keep things from getting messier for a bit, but it's not really fixing the leak, right? The leak stands for the behaviors or thoughts we're trying to change, and the bucket is like those quick, easy fixes we try. This shows us that real change means finding the underlying cause of the problem, not just dealing with what's on the surface.

Sometimes, we look for the effortless way out or want others to make us feel good to patch up our problems. It's like putting buckets all over the place, hoping to catch the water from a leaky roof. These might help for a little while, but they don't get to the heart of the issue. The true, lasting fix starts when we look inside ourselves.

Everything we need to fix our thoughts and feelings has been with us the whole time. The happiness and approval we're looking for are actually things we can give ourselves. It's our way of thinking that's in the way. When we realize this, we're ready to start repairing our "leaky roofs" properly.

We may discover that all the tools we need for mending, such as our thoughts and emotions, have been within us all along. Recognizing that the happiness and approval we seek can, in fact, be sourced from within—and that it's our perspective that often obstructs this realization—prepares us to effectively address our "leaky roofs." With this awareness, we're equipped to initiate the true repair process.

For example, in high school, a teen struggled to fit in, often changing her hobbies and style to match the popular crowd. Despite these efforts, she felt disconnected and unseen. One night, feeling particularly down, she talked to her parent about the struggle to belong.

Listening closely, the parent asked, "What interests you, even if nobody else seems to care about it?" Reflecting on this, the teen admitted her fascination with astronomy, a passion she'd sidelined to avoid standing out.

The teen decided to join the school's astronomy club, a small but welcoming group. Here, she discovered peers who shared her enthusiasm for the stars. Gradually, the teen formed genuine friendships based on shared interests, not on pretense.

This experience taught the teen a crucial lesson. True belonging doesn't come from conforming but from embracing and sharing one's genuine interests. This insight, fostered by a supportive conversation with her parent, helped the teen find her place and build authentic connections.

This leads us to turn our focus inward, growing our inner happiness instead of looking for outside solutions. It's about understanding how powerful our thoughts are in shaping how we feel and what we do. Taking charge of our thoughts and listening softly to our inner voice lets us begin a journey of real, meaningful change, moving our lives toward being more fulfilled and understanding ourselves.

For more tips and tools to help you and teens oversee thoughts and feelings, check out our resources. https://www.upliftingeducation.com/resources

FROGS: Navigating Teen Parenting

Parenting teens is like going on a hike through the wilderness. In this journey, the FROGS framework serves as our reliable map, guiding us through the varying terrains and challenges we encounter along the way.

G is for Grounding. Within the FROGS framework for parenting teens, grounding can be likened to the acceptance and acknowledgment that we may not have all the answers or know every twist and turn the trail might present. This element of the guide emphasizes the importance of authenticity and openness in our relationships with teens.

Being grounded means embracing the journey with a sense of realism and honesty, acknowledging our vulnerabilities, and admitting when we're unsure. This approach resonates deeply with teens, as it mirrors their own experiences of dealing with their problems. It reassures them that it's perfectly normal not to have everything figured out and that uncertainty is a part of growth and learning.[1]

Just as snacks and water sustain us physically on a hike, being grounded provides the emotional and psychological sustenance required. It fosters an environment of trust and understanding, where teens feel safe expressing their doubts and curiosities.

Grounding sets a foundation for open communication, where questions are encouraged and exploration is supported. It shows teens the value of self-reflection and self-acceptance, guiding them to discover their paths with confidence. By showing that even adults don't have all the answers, we model the lifelong process of learning and adapting. Steps, whether certain or uncertain, contribute to the richness of our journey together.

S is for Simple Conversations. Let's return to the wilderness metaphor. We're walking along a trail surrounded by nature's wonders. Every so often, we find a perfect spot to stop, take a deep breath, and soak in the view. It's in these pauses, these moments of quiet appreciation, that we find a chance to connect.

Sharing moments with our teens can be like these peaceful stops along the hike. It's not about having big, fancy conversations filled with complex words. Instead, it's about those simple, heart-to-heart chats where we listen to each other. These talks are the important aspect, where we show teens that they are important and that what they think and feel matters.

Think of it as speaking less and listening more. It's about opening up the space for teens to share their world without feeling the need to fill every silence with words. It's a chance to show them we're there, fully present, ready to listen to even the quietest whispers of their heart.

This doesn't mean we need to have all the answers or offer grand solutions. It's more about being there, showing that we care, and giving them the attention they deserve. It's these simple conversations, these shared moments of genuine connection, which can strengthen our bond. And who knows? Amidst the laughter and the lightness, we might stumble upon some profound insights together.

Such simple yet profound conversations can pave the way for significant insights, much like how stopping to look at the view can reveal landscapes we might otherwise miss if we were too focused on the destination. They foster an environment where teens can express their doubts, share their dreams, and navigate their challenges with the reassurance that they are not alone. Through these shared moments, we not only strengthen our bond with them but also encourage their journey.

The FROGS map with Flexibility, Rapport, Outcome, Grounding, and Simple Conversations helps us create a space where teens feel valued. Being flexible is like adjusting our path when the weather changes. Building rapport means walking side by side, showing we're in this together. Focusing on outcomes is like dreaming about the view from the top, not just the steps to get there. Grounded parenting shares wisdom from the roads we've already traveled. Simple Conversations are those meaningful chats that make the journey memorable.

This book isn't about guiding teens. It's about working together, making it easier and more meaningful for both parents and teens. Savannah's journey, from facing tough times as a teen to becoming a strong adult, gets us thinking. Every teen has a unique path. How can we recognize and celebrate teens' uniqueness and make an effort to provide the right kind of support?

Savannah's story isn't just a personal narrative. It's a lesson on the Inner Connection Quest, emphasizing the importance of looking inward for strength and guidance. It challenges us to ask how we can listen softly to our inner voice, embrace our true selves, and understand each other more deeply. It's about creating an environment where being authentic is valued and everyone is supported in finding their way. Through meaningful conversations, empathy, and unconditional support, we discover the resilience and joy that come from embracing our inner selves and the unique paths we all walk.

As we wrap up Savannah's story about finding strength and being true to oneself, we're stepping into PART II - WHOLE-SOME RELATIONSHIPS. We're about to learn how we can help teens make real, strong friendships that make them happy and healthy. Get ready to hear about how we can connect with others in a way that brings out the best in everyone.

PART TWO
WHOLESOME RELATIONSHIPS

The Inner Connection Quest is a journey that brings more joy into our lives and strengthens our relationships with others. It teaches us how to quiet our busy minds so that our inner wisdom can guide our daily actions. Along the way, we learn to understand and show genuine empathy and love to others. This path focuses on creating uplifting connections that increase happiness for us and those around us. Through this process, we realize how valuable good relationships are in boosting our overall well-being and happiness.

THE BASICS

In Compton, California, two sisters, Venus and Serena Williams, started an amazing journey. They grew up dreaming big, aiming to rock the tennis world. From the start, they were both teammates and friendly rivals, sharing everything from their dreams to the tennis court they practiced on. They were different in many ways but had one big goal together: to become the top tennis players on the planet. This story is all about the real-life adventures of the famous Williams sisters.

Sister Squad

From their laid-back beginnings under the sunny California skies to the grandeur of the world's elite tennis tournaments, Venus and Serena Williams' journey is a heartwarming tale of sisterhood, competition, and unwavering support. Off the court, they were each other's biggest fans, but once they stepped onto the court, they transformed into competitors, each with her eyes on the prize.

At the 1997 U.S. Open, Venus emerged as the new sensation,

while Serena, not competing, was her biggest cheerleader from the sidelines. Serena would say, "I'm so pumped! It's like I'm out there playing too."[1] This moment highlighted their incredible bond, even as they reached for the same dreams.

Their path together resembled a dance—mostly graceful, with occasional missteps. Facing each other across the net, their sisterly connection remained strong, unshaken by the competitive storm. Serena once reflected, "The toughest part? It's not the match. It's navigating my emotions afterwards." Her words reveal the complex mix of love for Venus and her own ambition.

Venus echoed this sentiment in 2001, saying, "I always cheer for Serena, which is hard when I need to win against her." Their rivalry on the court never overshadowed their mutual admiration and love, displaying a bond that went beyond trophies and titles.

Their connection went beyond sports. They shared dreams, a home, and even career paths. When Serena launched her fashion line, Venus supported her sister's passion beyond tennis. "She's been my rock through the fashion shows, new lines, my complaints and challenges," Serena could say, showing how deep their relationship was.

Parents commonly hope their kids share a loving and supportive bond strong enough to oversee rivalry and competition. Research tells us family relationships are key for teens, leading to better mental health and success at school.[2]

Think about dinners where families catch up after their day. Whether it's a feast we've whipped up or a quick meal we've grabbed from somewhere, these gatherings are so much more than just eating occasions. They're where we share laughs, swap stories, and show our love for each other.

Take family game night as an example. It's not just fun and games. It's a lesson in living. It's where we learn to be okay with not consistently winning, to be humble when we do win, and to find joy in just being together. Without even realizing it, teens are soaking up lessons on love, respect, and how to draw lines in the most enjoyable way.

Then there are the tougher times, like when teens go through a rough challenge. These moments are golden for us to show them how much we care. It's in these times that we can exhibit empathy, support, and the strength of our family bond.

Next, we're delving into the good stuff, like how to boost emotional growth, level up our communication game, deepen love and tighten connections. Sure, there's a mountain of books out there on this, but think of this chapter as your secret quick start for crafting supportive relationships.

Breaking the Ice

Scene: A cluttered living room, late evening. The tension is as thick as the plot of the latest binge-worthy series. Alex, clutching a worn-out soccer ball, hesitates by the door. Sprawled on the couch, Jake is lost in his phone screen's glow.

Alex (*voice shaky*): "Hey, Jake... Can we talk? Like, actually talk?"

Jake (*looks up, surprised*): "Uh, sure... What's up?"

Alex (*takes a deep breath*): "I know things have been, like, super weird between us. And I... I miss hanging out. Remember when we used to play until 3 AM, laughing so hard our stomachs hurt?"

Jake (*a half-smile cracking his previously indifferent facade*): "Yeah, I remember. Those were great times. But I thought you were too cool for your dorky brother now."

Alex (*shuffles closer, the soccer ball now forgotten*): "Nah, man. I've just been... stuck, I guess."

Jake (*sitting up, interest piqued*): "So, what's been going on?"

Alex (*laughs, the sound lighter than it's been in weeks*): "Just school and stuff. Feeling like I'm supposed to have it all figured out, you know?"

Jake (*nods*): "Totally get it. I've been there."

Alex: "Exactly! But talking to you... it's better. Maybe we don't have to have everything sorted. Maybe it's okay to just be... us."

Jake: "Yeah, being real is better than pretending to have it all together. Plus, facing stuff is easier when you're not alone."

Alex: "Can we start over? Maybe team up like old times?"

Jake: "Sure. But first, how about we conquer the final boss in Dark Shadows?"

Alex: "You're on. And hey, thanks for listening."

[The room fills with the sound of laughter. The brothers find common ground in shared fears and dreams. The conversation isn't perfect, but it's a start. A testament to the power of reaching out, finding empathy in shared struggles, and rebuilding connections one word at a time.]

Moral of the Story: Sometimes, the most daunting conversations can lead to the most unexpected bridges between hearts.

————

This story about Alex and Jake isn't just a sweet moment between brothers. It's a hint for us on how to help teens get along better. It shows us how important it is for families to talk openly and listen to each other.

When Alex stands at the door, unsure if he should talk to Jake, it's like watching a scene we know too well. Teens often want to reach out but might worry they'll get brushed off. When Jake looks up, surprised but willing to chat, it reminds us that most of the time, teens are open to connecting. They need to know it's okay.

For us, this means making sure our home is a place where everyone feels comfortable sharing their thoughts. It's about letting our kids know it's okay to talk about anything, from school stress to friendship and drama, without getting judged.

The chat between the brothers shows us another point. Sometimes, the stuff that bugs us isn't super serious, but talking it out can make an enormous difference. Catching these trivial things early can stop them from turning into bigger issues.

Plus, remembering the good times, like late-night game sessions, can remind siblings (and everyone in the family) of the fun they have together. This can be a bridge back to those close feelings.

Bridging Worlds with the FROGS Map

In our journey as parents, finding ways to connect deeply with teens amid the allure of screens can be an intimidating task. The FROGS map provides a framework for us to navigate these challenges together, uncovering a space where teens feel seen and heard.

Demonstrating flexibility in our approach allows us to engage with our teens from a place of understanding and respect for their digital interests. Initiating dialogue with genuine curiosity can make a world of difference. "I've noticed the time you spend with your devices, and I'm genuinely curious about what draws you in. Would you mind sharing with me?" This shows our openness to their perspective and an eagerness to understand their digital world.

To build rapport, we express a sincere interest in their online activities. Rather than dismissing their screen time, we can invite them to share their digital experiences with us. "We'd really like to understand why you enjoy [specific game or app]. Could we explore it together sometime?" This gesture of wanting to be part of their digital life can help strengthen our bond.

Our outcome can be to foster a meaningful connection, focusing on shared experiences that bring us closer. Suggesting activities that cater to mutual interests can encourage spending quality time together away from screens. "How about we try something new this weekend, something we can both enjoy? A hike, a board game, or a creative project? What do you think?" Keeping our sights on enhancing our relationship guides our interactions toward fulfilling and enjoyable times together.

Grounding our interactions in personal insight and experience is crucial. Before offering advice, we ask if it's welcome, showing respect for teens' autonomy. This validates their independence and frames our advice as something offered from a place of empathy and understanding rather than a directive.

Parent: "Hey, I remember feeling overwhelmed at your age, juggling school, friends, and activities. I found some ways to balance it all. Can I share?"

Teen: "Sure, I guess."

Parent: "You know, feeling swamped with choices isn't new. Happened to me, too. I figured out that mixing activities like reading or hiking with my screen time really helped. What about you? Any hobbies you're curious about picking up?"

We can initiate simple conversations that encourage openness and sharing. Asking open-ended questions about their day, thoughts, or feelings invites them into a dialogue. "How was your day? Anything interesting happen [online or offline]?" This sets the stage for a two-way conversation. The question isn't as important as our heart to reach out.

By integrating the FROGS map into our interactions, we emphasize an approach rooted in flexibility, mutual respect, shared outcomes, personal grounding, and open dialogue. This way respects teens' independence and digital engagement. It fosters a deeper, more meaningful connection by sharing personal insights, always with permission, ensuring our advice is welcomed and valued.

· · ·

Teamwork Makes the Dream Work

Imagine the teen years as being part of a dynamic duo in an epic video game, where working together is the key to success. It's a bit like the legendary Venus and Serena Williams, whose teamwork both on and off the court is inspiring. Now, let's zoom into the world of Nan and Lily, two high school students who are as different as can be. Nan is the chill type who likes to take in the scenery, while Lily is all about making every day a vibrant, action-packed adventure.

Despite their differences, Nan and Lily both like science, which becomes their secret language, much like tennis for Venus and Serena. This shared passion turns them from an unlikely pair into science project superstars.

Sure, they hit some bumps along the way. They had their disagreements, like who had the better idea for their project, and they even got a bit competitive at times. When Lily had to move away for a while, it seemed like their team might be heading for an end. However, just like the Williams sisters, these challenges only made their friendship stronger. They learned to listen to each other, find common ground, and let their competitive spirit bring them closer rather than drive them apart. Even miles apart, they stayed connected through messages and the occasional heartfelt letter.

When Lily returned, their friendship was stronger than ever, proving that it wasn't just their love for science that kept them close. It was their mutual respect, their ability to talk things out, and their shared experiences of overcoming obstacles together that truly solidified their bond. Strong relationships are built on more than only common interests. They thrive on resilience through disagreements, support during competition, and staying connected, no matter what the physical distance is. Nurturing these bonds with respect, open communication, and a willingness to face challenges together is what turns them into a source of strength and joy in our lives.

Unpacking Wisdom

Let's explore a concept that deeply resonated with me, inspired by Beverley Wilson Hayes in the "Going Deeper" video from my Innate Wellness Specialist Certification Course.[3] The four pivotal stages of acquiring and imparting knowledge are: Gathering the Pieces, Feeling the Knowledge, Living It, and Sharing My Journey. I'll illustrate this using my experience with weight loss.

Gathering the Pieces: I started by absorbing all the facts and advice on weight loss I could. I read books, watched countless videos, and gathered information from blogs. It felt like I was gearing up for a big project, equipped with all the necessary tools. But at this stage, it's just a collection of pieces waiting to be assembled.

Feeling the Knowledge: This is where the transformation begins. I progressed from merely knowing stuff about weight loss to feeling it deeply. It's one thing to grasp the science of nutrition and quite another to realize what healthy eating and being active do for me on a personal level. The moment I chose healthier options, not because a chart told me to but because I genuinely felt better, was when wisdom started to resonate within me. The vision was forming in my heart and mind.

· · ·

Living It: Here's where the magic happens. I start to apply everything I've learned about weight loss to my daily life. It's not just about shedding pounds. It's about how I feel, the confidence I gain, and the energy I discover. This step is when knowledge comes to life. It's the difference between understanding how to swim theoretically and actually jumping into the water. I'm not just talking the talk. I'm walking the walk and gradually manifesting the vision in my heart about it. As of this time, while drafting this book, I'm on this step, working it out day by day.

Sharing My Journey: After going through the process, from learning to living it, I'll be in a place to share my journey authentically. My insights will carry a different weight because I'm not just repeating information. The wisdom I share will be my lived experiences. It'll be guiding others on the path to weight loss only after I've traveled it myself. My advice will come from a place of genuine grounding.

Parallel to this journey is the importance of listening. It's transformative to listen softly by turning down the external noise to reach a place of quiet. It's about carefully tuning in and focusing on what's going on inside us. When the entire world seems to be shouting what we should do, the secret is to listen to our inner voice.

This inner listening not only prepares us for personal growth but also sets the stage for resolutions. Forgiveness acts like a silencer for the noise of anger and hurt, allowing us to move forward feeling lighter and more open to new beginnings. It's about being filled with unconditional love, creating a powerful ripple effect that can extend beyond the individual and relationships to influence larger communities and even international relations.

· · ·

Forgiveness and Wisdom

In 1991, Reverend Sun Myung Moon and Mrs. Hak Ja Han Moon undertook a remarkable journey to North Korea, a move filled with deep personal and political significance. Both were born in North Korea, and having fled to the South as refugees, their return was not just a diplomatic mission but an intense homecoming. Despite the painful memories and the stark opposition between their beliefs and the communist regime of Kim Il Sung, they embarked on this journey with a mission of peace and reconciliation at heart.

This trip was a testament to their incredible capacity for forgiveness. Having personally suffered under the harsh conditions of their homeland, including torture and imprisonment, both Rev. Moon and Mrs. Moon had every reason to harbor resentment. Yet, they chose a different path. By clearing their hearts of any bitterness and tuning into their deep inner wisdom, they demonstrated an extraordinary commitment to healing and understanding. Their decision to return to the place of their birth and suffering, not with a message of retribution but with one of reconciliation, underscores the impact of listening to one's inner voice of compassion and empathy.

Their warm discussions with Kim Il Sung on topics ranging from reunification to global peace were steps to lay the groundwork for a future of cooperation and peace. This wasn't merely about political negotiation. It was a daring act to mend a fractured relationship, showing that even the deepest divides could be overcome with heartfelt dialogue and a willingness to forgive.

For parents today, the Moons' story offers powerful lessons in connecting with teens. It reminds us that listening deeply to our innermost wisdom can transform our relationships. Just as the Moons returned to their birthplace with open hearts, parents can approach misunderstandings or conflicts with teens from a place of inner clarity and compassion. This kind of listening goes beyond surface-level communication. It's about genuinely understanding and empathizing with teens' experiences and emotions.

In addition, by embodying forgiveness and empathy, as the Moons did so courageously, parents can convey to teens invaluable lessons about handling personal grievances and disagreements. It shows them the strength in forgiveness and the importance of clearing one's heart of resentment to move forward with openness and a peaceful countenance.

Parents can foster an environment of open communication and mutual respect at home. By delving deep into our inner wisdom and heart, we can create stronger, more loving relationships with teens. This not only brings peace within our families but also equips kids with the emotional intelligence to build healthy relationships throughout their lives.

Hear in Heart

Listening softly is about tuning in with our hearts and listening to more than just words. When we share our struggles or successes, we're not just exchanging information. We're feeling and connecting with another person on a level that goes beyond the surface. This kind of listening can change how we perceive things, offering new insights and deeper empathy.

Beverley Wilson Hayes summed it up beautifully: "There's an ear in learn, hear, and heart. There's also art in the word heart. So, learn to hear in your heart because that's the art of listening."

As we navigate our own paths, whether in reconciliation, weight loss, or in any endeavor, remembering these steps to learning and the power of listening softly can guide us from casual knowledge to profound wisdom and connection. It's about integrating what we know into what we feel and do, and then sharing that journey with authenticity and heart.

As we wrap up this chapter, think of our journey with teens not just as daily talks about screen time or chores but as a path filled with laughs, sensitive awareness, and growing together.

Imagine building a family life that's as unforgettable and meaningful as winning a big tennis match. It's not just the highs of victory but also the tough times that test us. It's about seeing the beauty in both the good and challenging times, knowing that it's all part of a larger journey we're on together. How can we make sure everyone knows they're an important part of the team, especially when things get tough?

On this journey to connect more, our vision is to make every moment count, turning our family time into a collection of awesome experiences. How do we make sure this trip is not just about the end game but about enjoying the steps we walk together? It's in these moments, through difficulties, that we write our family's story, a tale of sticking together, facing challenges head-on, and always having each other's backs.

The Inner Connection Quest is a shared adventure, a journey that binds us together as we travel through life's difficulties. It invites us to dive deep into the heart of what it means to be a family, fostering a delicate awareness of our own emotions and those of the people we hold dear. Together, we embark on this path, not just to smooth over the rough edges, but to forge an unbreakable bond that supports dreams and manages challenges with unity. It's like being part of a team where everyone plays their part in clinching the championship. Cheers, activities, and efforts matter.

Committing to this quest does more than just enhance our present day to day life. It lays down a foundation for a family legacy built on resilience, sensitivity, and an enjoyable sense of togetherness. Through this journey, we learn to tune into the delicate rhythms of each other's hearts, creating a symphony of support that can weather any storm.

When you are ready to move on, we'll step into "Beneath the Surface." Here, we'll hear Isabella's story. Through her journey and a touching letter from her great-grandmother, we'll dive into themes like bouncing back, finding out who we are, and the deep connections that shape us. Let's follow Isabella as she shows us that there's a chance to grow and understand ourselves beneath our challenges.

CHAPTER 6
BENEATH THE SURFACE

Isabella's sneakers pressed into the freshly mown grass. Each step echoed memories. She moved fluidly, seamlessly merging with the pace of the soccer ball as it bounced between her feet. For onlookers, it was simply a showcase of athleticism. But for Isabella, the soccer field was a canvas of dreams, hopes, and memories.

She paused at the end of the field, her breaths deep and rhythmic. As her fingers lightly touched the turf, she murmured to herself, "Right here, my first goal." Moving to the middle side, she bent down, retying her shoelace. The simple act was layered with cherished memories of pregame rituals in that very spot.

Days later, the hustle chatter of excited students filled the corridor. Eyes darted over the selection list, searching for familiar names. Isabella approached with a palpable mix of hope and anxiety. But her name was absent. The noise around her faded, replaced by a dull ringing in her ears. She felt a tight grip on her arm.

"It's just a list, Isabella," consoled her best friend. But both knew it wasn't 'just' anything for Isabella.

Home offered little comfort. The walls that once served as the backdrop to Isabella's cheerful recounts of soccer practice now stood witness to her stifled sobs and silent dinners. She retreated to her room to be alone with her thoughts, wrestling with the sting of disappointment and longing for a familiar sense of accomplishment that seemed just out of reach.

One evening, her younger brother Logan peeked into her room, concern etched in his eyes. "Want to stargaze tonight?" he asked. She merely shook her head, the weight of her disappointment hanging heavily around her.

Another evening, as a warm breeze drifted through the house, Isabella's mother, Jane, approached her. 'Let's take a walk,' she suggested gently.

In Rosewood Park, Isabella inhaled deeply, letting the fresh scent of nature fill her lungs. "I've always loved it here," she murmured, eyes scanning the lush greenery.

Jane smiled. "It has a certain magic, doesn't it?" She paused to listen to the distant chirping of birds.

Isabella's eyes wandered. "Mom, it's tough, you know? Everywhere I look, someone's doing better, looking better, being more..."

Jane pulled Isabella close. "You're wonderful, Isabella. Life isn't about ticking off achievements. Watching you blossom into the person you are has been the greatest joy of my life."

She paused their walk and reached into her bag, extracting an aged envelope from a hidden pocket. The paper was a soft cream, its edges slightly frayed. "This," she began, gently caressing the envelope's surface, "is a letter your great-grandmother wrote to me."

Isabella took the envelope and carefully unfolded the well-worn paper. As she read, the world around her blurred. The words were more than just ink on paper. They pulsated with life. The wisdom came not from textbooks or scholars but from a life richly lived, lessons hard learned, and a heart that knew boundless love.

———

Dear Jane,

As the sun sets on our family home, I'm reminded of the young girl who chased dreams beneath the old elm tree. I've seen you grow into a remarkable young woman, and lately, I sense you questioning your place in this vast world, just like when you missed that theater production role and doubted your worth.

There will be times when you doubt how much you matter, especially when things don't go your way and it feels like your successes are hidden behind your mistakes. But don't forget, your true value isn't about winning all the time or the bumps along the road.

Your real worth, Jane, shines through in the joy your laughter brings to those around you, how you're there for friends when they need someone to lean on, and, most of all, in what makes you one-of-a-kind. In this big, wide world, you have a special spot, my dear, that perfectly reflects the beauty of life itself.

With all the love a heart can hold,
Grandma

———

That magical day in Rosewood Park, filled with the gentle wisdom and love of her great-grandmother's letter, had ignited a fire in Isabella's heart. When she received an assignment in her Advanced Literature course to create an oral history project focused on family stories and legacies, she realized it was the perfect opportunity to explore the similarities and differences between the women of earlier generations and today.

Driven by this newfound curiosity, Isabella turned first to her mother, eager to understand how her mom felt as a teenager and the challenges she faced. Isabella set out to collect these stories and weave them into a project that captured each generation's unique struggles and successes. For her, this was more than just an assignment or a trip down memory lane. It was a chance to see how values have changed, how hopes are shared, and how the bonds between generations connect us all.

The Recorded Chronicles

In the quiet solitude of her room, Isabella settled cross-legged on the carpeted floor with handwritten notes, color-coded pens, and a frayed journal encircling her. With its blinking red light, the voice recorder awaited its role in the center of this space.

The notes were pieces of a larger puzzle she aimed to complete. She envisioned this interview as a portal offering raw, unfiltered glimpses into the past.

Taking a deep breath, she called, "Ready, Mom?"

Jane entered the room with a comforting cup of tea, warming her hands. She took a moment to glance at the scattered notes before settling gracefully onto the plush chair, offering an affirmative nod.

The room was momentarily suspended in a silent reverence. Then, with a gentle press, Isabella activated the voice recorder, marking the beginning of their shared journey into the past.

Understanding the Adolescent Brain

Isabella, leaning forward: "Mom, were there times as a teen when you felt like your brain was just... all over the place?"

Jane, with a chuckle: "Absolutely, Isabella. Some days felt like a rollercoaster. One moment, I'd be soaring, thrilled about a good grade or a shared joke, and the next, I'd plummet, devastated by a petty argument with a friend. It was an era of intense highs and lows. In retrospect, it was a natural part of growing up."

Isabella's brows furrowed in curiosity: "I've read about our brains going through this strange 'clean-up' phase during our teen years. Did you ever sense that happening?"

Jane, pausing thoughtfully: "In hindsight, I think I did. Some friendships drifted away, interests shifted, and hobbies I moved past. I guess you could say it was my mind's way of creating space for fresh experiences and insights."

Isabella, fiddling with the hem of her shirt: "Mom, did your perspective change a lot when you were growing up, especially when things got tough?"

Jane smiled and nodded. "Oh, for sure. Both the challenges and the good moments shaped how I saw the world. Books made me question things I took for granted, I met people who opened my eyes, and those tough times made me stronger."

————

Although we once thought the brain was mostly set by childhood, it actually keeps evolving into our twenties. This includes a cleanup phase, where the brain strengthens meaningful connections and removes less-used ones.

Dr. Jay Giedd, a leading expert, describes this as an "adaptive fine-tuning."[1] It's as if the brain is an orchestra conductor, meticulously fine-tuning each section to achieve the perfect harmony. This phase is particularly crucial for the areas of the brain responsible for decision-making and impulse control, which are still maturing in adolescents. This developmental curve helps to shed light on the often unpredictable emotional landscape teens navigate, where profound insight can abruptly give way to spontaneous decisions.

This transformative phase isn't solely defined by emotional turbulence. It also primes the adolescent brain for remarkable learning and creativity. This is a pivotal time for teens to harness their experiences, shaping their character and wisdom in profound ways. It's an unparalleled period of growth, where challenges and opportunities alike contribute to the development of a rich personality.

Empathy and Connection

Isabella's hesitant yet curious voice continued, "Were there moments when you felt pressured to be someone you weren't, especially with friends or at school?"

Jane's eyes clouded momentarily with memories. "Without a doubt. Peer pressure isn't a new concept," she replied, taking a moment to sip her tea. "Wanting to fit in, to be part of the 'cool crowd,' made me act in odd ways. Sometimes, I laughed at jokes I didn't find funny or went along with plans I disagreed with just to feel accepted."

Taking a deep breath, Isabella asked, "How did you find your way? How did you learn to be genuine?"

Jane said. "Life has a way of teaching us. With time, I realized those acts were exhausting." She leaned back. "It took a few hard lessons. But I learned that the relationships worth cherishing were those where I could just be myself."

Isabella's fingers fidgeted. "It's reassuring to know that these struggles aren't just mine. Did these experiences change your relationships in any way?"

Jane nodded. "The friends I treasure most today are those who saw through my disguises and stood by me through thick and thin. Those trials helped me differentiate between fleeting acquaintances and lifelong friends."

Shifting slightly, Isabella's gaze landed on a nearby family photo, their smiles captured forever. She glanced back at her mom, admiration in her voice: "Mom, you've been through so much. It's cool to see how strong you are now. You're pretty awesome."

———

Isabella and Jane's conversation reveals the common teen challenges of self-identity amidst peer dynamics. This aligns with Blakemore's research,[2] which details the transformations in the adolescent brain, particularly in areas governing social behaviors. Four areas are worth summarizing.

Social Sensitivity Spike: Imagine a teen's brain is like a social radar, suddenly turning up to maximum sensitivity. This is because areas of the brain involved in understanding others' thoughts and feelings become more active. For example, suppose a teen posts a photo on social media. In that case, they might be hyper-aware of every like, comment, or lack thereof, interpreting these as direct reflections of their social standing.

Risk and Reward Rebalancing: The adolescent brain undergoes changes in how it manages risk and rewards. Teens might be more likely to take risks, like trying a challenging skateboard trick or staying up late on a school night, because the thrill of the moment often outweighs potential consequences in their minds. This is tied to developing the brain's reward system, which is hitting the gas pedal on seeking exciting experiences.

Emotional Intensity: The parts of the brain that process emotions are also evolving. This can make emotions feel more intense. For a teen, a disagreement with a friend might not just feel like a minor spat. It could feel like the end of the world. This heightened emotional experience is part of the brain's development journey.

Identity Exploration: The prefrontal cortex, which is like the brain's decision-making captain, is still maturing. This means teens are naturally inclined to explore and experiment with different identities, interests, and beliefs. It's like their brain is encouraging them to try on different hats to see which one fits best, whether that's joining a new club at school or experimenting with unique styles of music.

What's fascinating is that despite the whirlwind of changes in society and the unique challenges every generation faces, the core experiences of growing up, like the struggle for identity and the desire to fit in, remain remarkably constant. These changes affect how teens see themselves and their place in the social world, guiding them toward more meaningful connections.

Exploration and Identity

Isabella continued, "Grandma always amuses me with tales of your teen years." She chuckled, her eyes shining with mischief. "Did trying all those crazy things help you figure out who you were?"

Jane's laugh was hearty and genuine, filling the room with warmth. She leaned forward. "Oh, your grandmother remembers too much!" She added, "I explored quite a bit. I dabbled in painting. The attic still has some of my 'masterpieces.' I became part of various clubs, and" she leaned closer, lowering her voice for effect, "I even wrote some poetry. But that's our little secret, okay?" She chuckled softly.

From the corner of the room, the soft ticking of the grandfather clock provided a rhythmic backdrop to their conversation. Isabella asked, "Everyone keeps talking about how teens are always trying to figure themselves out. Did you also go through that whole 'Who am I?' thing?"

Jane traced a finger along the rim of her teacup, lost in thought. After a moment, she began speaking slowly, choosing her words carefully. "Imagine standing at the center of a big maze, with lots of paths going in all different directions. Each path represents a different version of who you might become. You'll feel excited and curious to explore but also a little uncertain and confused sometimes." She looked directly into Isabella's eyes, and they shared a silent understanding. "And that's okay. Growing up is about exploring, making mistakes, and figuring things out. It's all part of your journey to discovering who you are."

———

Jane's teen years were an adventure as she tried to understand who she was, a stage that psychologist Erik Erikson called "Identity vs. Role Confusion."[3] She explored painting, joined clubs, and wrote poetry, all while feeling pressure to meet others' expectations. Despite the challenging journey, Jane learned that being true to herself was crucial. She found her true passions and the friends who mattered most, helping her grow more confident in herself.

Jane was unaware of a simpler path that could have eased her journey, rooted in Sydney Banks' "Three Principles: Mind, Consciousness, and Thought."[4] This framework suggests that our thoughts shape our feelings and perceptions of the world. Had she known these principles, she might have seen her creative pursuits not just as roles to experiment with but as genuine expressions of her individuality.

She would have realized that her emotions stemmed from her thoughts, much like how ripples spread across a still pond. Recognizing how these ripples shaped her perception, Jane might have better understood the discomfort of trying to fit into someone else's mold. Instead, she could have pictured herself as an artist shaping her own sculpture, carefully chiseling away unnecessary layers to reveal her authentic self underneath. This insight could have empowered her to confidently embrace her true identity, transforming her journey into a smoother, more fulfilling exploration of who she really is.

Parents can help teens navigate this journey by creating a supportive environment where individuality is encouraged, providing a safe space for self-expression without judgment. They can listen attentively to their teens' dreams and concerns and offer guidance rooted in understanding rather than imposing expectations. Helping them see the importance of internal reflection and positive self-talk can foster the confidence to shape their own paths. By consistently reinforcing that it's perfectly fine to be themselves, parents can enable their teens to embrace their authentic identities, regardless of external pressures.

Sense of Worth

Isabella gazed contemplatively. "Mom, did you ever get this weird feeling, like... there's something bigger out there guiding us? I can't really put it into words, but it's kind of comforting, you know?"

Jane nodded. "I've felt that too. I've often sensed a connection to something greater, a web of existence that binds us all. It's like the quiet whispers of the universe, offering subtle guidance."

"For instance," Jane continued, her eyes distant yet sparkling with memories, "when I was around your age, I'd visit the old elm tree at the back of our house. I'd sit under its sprawling branches, feel the gentle sway of the leaves, and listen to the birds' chorus. In those moments, it felt like I was connected to something bigger, a shared experience of nature and life that showed we were all deeply linked."

Isabella smiled softly, reminiscing about her own moments of connection. "I had this feeling after a super tough soccer game. Honestly, the score wasn't even the thing. It was more about how we all came together as a team. Passes, goals, and shouts felt like it was about more than just the game. It wasn't just about winning; it felt like we were all in it together, like a real bond with everyone out there."

Jane's eyes gleamed with pride. "That's beautiful, Isabella. It's these moments that help us find our inner value. We realize that we're not just isolated beings but threads in a vast tapestry woven together with meaning and intention. Our worth isn't just our individual achievements or setbacks but our place in this grand design."

Isabella leaned back, absorbing her mother's words. "It's kind of reassuring. Even when things get tough, or I feel alone, there's this bigger story we're all part of."

The two sat in silent reflection, letting the weight of the conversation settle in. The room seemed to pulse with gentle energy, echoing the timeless rhythm of life, connection, and the quest for deeper understanding.

———

Isabella and Jane's conversation delves deeply into the heart of what it means to be human. Together, they unravel a story that redefines our understanding of self-worth, revealing a powerful truth: our value isn't solely about personal triumphs. Instead, it's woven into the rhythms of our relationships, the depth of shared experiences, and the profound realization that we are all part of a larger, magnificent tapestry.

Discovering our sense of worth becomes an adventure when we

carefully listen to the quiet stirrings within. This gentle, attentive listening illuminates our unique place in the world, revealing the beauty and significance of our existence in the grand scheme of things. By tuning in with empathy and openness, we allow our intrinsic value to shine like a newly discovered constellation, highlighting the unique contribution and significance of our presence in the cosmos.

The Cinema of the Mind

Isabella's journey, marked by the experiences of her teen years, mirrored the ever-changing scenes in the cinema of her mind. Just as she mastered the soccer field, she began to learn the art of navigating her thoughts, a skill far more intricate and vital.

One evening, Isabella and her mother took their usual walk to Rosewood Park. As they settled on their favorite bench, Isabella's mind was like a cinema playing a relentless series of movies—scenes of missed opportunities, comparisons with others, and harsh self-judgment. Each thought was like a frame in a film projected onto the screen of her consciousness.

Jane, recognizing the turmoil in her daughter, decided to share a metaphor that had recently helped her. "Imagine your mind is like a cinema," she began. "The thoughts you have are movies playing on its screen. Sometimes these movies are happy, sometimes sad, and sometimes they're scary or upsetting."

Isabella listened, her eyes reflecting the flickering images of her own 'mental movies.'

"But here's the thing," Jane continued, "just like in a real cinema, you have the choice. If you don't like the movie, you can walk out. You don't have to sit there and watch it. The projector of thoughts will keep running, but you don't have to be its captive audience."

The concept resonated with Isabella. She realized she had the power to 'walk out' of her mental cinema's unhelpful screenings. She couldn't stop the flow of thoughts but learned to disengage or choose how she reacted to them. While thoughts are inevitable, engaging with them is a choice. This insight helped her manage her emotions more effectively, marking a significant step in her personal growth.

Isabella's experiences, underscored by her mother's wisdom and her grandmother's letter's timeless counsel, illuminate the path toward embracing inner worth. It's a journey marked not by the destinations reached but by the insights gained, the connections deepened, and the resilience forged. From the soccer field to the quiet moments in Rosewood Park, each chapter of Isabella's journey reflects the universal quest for identity, belonging, and understanding in the whirlwind of adolescence.

Embarking on the Inner Connection Quest with teens is like guiding them through the intricate "cinema of the mind." This voyage enlightens them on their inherent ability to sift through their thoughts, choosing which to embrace and which to release. This is crucial for navigating challenging emotions and fostering resilience. It's as if we're handing them the director's chair for their mental narratives, enabling them to craft stories that strengthen confidence and well-being. Such a step is essential in stimulating their inner resilience, making their journey of self-discovery rewarding.

Helping teens to listen softly to the wisdom they have inside to get through tough times is a big part of the Inner Connection Quest. By talking about how everyone's experiences add up to something bigger, we can help them see how their own challenges and victories are critical. It shows them that they're not alone. They're part of the bigger picture, contributing to the world in their own way. This helps teens feel proud of who they are and brave enough to face anything.

As we close this chapter, let's value the lessons of empathy, connection, and the remarkable power of our inner wisdom. Let's honor the adolescent journey, with all its highs and lows, recognizing that within every teen lies the potential and the wisdom to grow into incredible individuals.

Each step, misstep, and achievement plants the seeds for their extraordinary development. This journey through their formative years isn't about the destination but about realizing the innate strength, resilience, and beauty they possess, ready to emerge in its own perfect time. It would be valuable to take some time to reflect on this chapter.

Next up, "Nurturing Authentic Love" will take us into some important conversations. It's about looking past what everyone else is doing and finding what makes a relationship valuable. Join us as the Anderson Family explores what it means to love authentically, setting the stage for meaningful connections.

CHAPTER 7

NURTURING AUTHENTIC LOVE

The Anderson family sat around their rustic dining table while an air of contemplation filled the room. Emma, 16, and her younger brother, Max, 14, listened as their parents, Sarah and David, brought up a topic often avoided, understanding and nurturing authentic love.

Sarah, a high school counselor, knew the importance of honest conversation. "Love isn't just about feelings," she started, gently stirring her tea. "It's about understanding yourself and the other person. It's about respect and dignity."

David nodded in agreement, "It's about making choices that honor you and the people you care about. Love should make you feel good about yourself."

Emma rolled her eyes slightly, a mix of skepticism and curiosity in her voice. "That sounds great and all, but at school, it's not like that. Everyone's just into dating for fun. It's... complicated."

Max, fidgeting with his napkin, added, "And online, everyone's showing off their relationships. If you're not with someone, it feels like you're missing out or something."

Sarah leaned forward. "I get it. There's a lot of pressure to fit in.

But remember, the best relationships are about more than just looking good on the outside. They're about really connecting with someone, understanding them, and feeling respected."

———

When the 1960s sexual revolution rolled in, it was like a massive wave promising boundless freedom and joy. Yet, beneath that thrilling crest, hidden challenges lurked. This era ushered in numerous freedoms, which sounded exciting. The problem was that it occasionally overlooked the elements of connection, responsibility, and respect.

Think about the idea of "free love." It's pretty attractive, especially to teens who are all about exploring new things. However, this idea tended to overlook the complicated emotions and results of intimate relationships. A lot of teens jump into these experiences without really knowing what they're getting into, leading to feelings of regret, being vulnerable, or even feeling let down. And it's not just about things like health risks or surprise pregnancies. It goes deeper, touching how someone feels about themselves and can leave emotional marks that last a long time.

Imagine a world where teens, with their parents' support, can look beyond what society expects. They build relationships based on a responsible attitude and shared values. In this world, the freedom that the sexual revolution promised gets a new meaning. It's not about chasing every whim but about knowing the true nature of love within us and others. Intimate relationships are spaces for growing together, infused with a mutually caring, long-term love.

Guardians of Love's Legacy

The Andersons were on one of their regular weekend hikes, a

tradition that always brought them closer to nature and each other. The trail was peaceful, surrounded by the vibrant greens and browns of the forest. It was here, amidst the tranquility of nature, that their conversations often delved deeper.

David, leading the way, turned back to his family with a reflective look. "You know, when I was your age, I had a pretty skewed idea of what love was," he began, his voice echoing slightly in the open space.

Emma, walking alongside Max, looked up with interest. "What do you mean, Dad?"

David chuckled softly. "Well, I thought love was all about grand gestures and intense emotions. I believed the movies, you know? That love was all about dramatic declarations and doing crazy things for attention."

Sarah smiled, joining in. "And then?"

"And then, I met your mom," David said, his eyes meeting Sarah's. "And I learned that real love is about the quiet moments, the everyday things. It's about being there for each other and being patient."

Max, who was usually more interested in the nature around him than family talks, was intrigued. "So, it's not like the movies?" he asked with a hint of sarcasm.

"No, not really," David replied. "Movies and social media often show just one side of love – the exciting, dramatic side. But they don't always show the important parts, like trust, support, and respect."

Emma asked, "But isn't the exciting part important too?"

"It is," Sarah interjected, "but it's not the starting point. A foundation of love is built on something deeper like consideration, shared commitment, and genuinely enjoying each other's company."

The trail opened up to a clearing, and the family took a moment to rest, sitting on a fallen log.

David leaned forward, looking at Emma and Max earnestly. "I want you both to know that waiting for that kind of love is okay. The kind that's built on something real, not just the thrill of the moment."

Emma nodded slowly, processing her father's words. "I guess it's like this hike. The exciting part is reaching the top, but the real experience is the walk itself, the stuff we see and talk about along the way."

"Exactly," David said, pleased. "And just like this hike, in relationships, you'll have difficulties. The important thing is to keep walking together, supporting each other."

Max, now looking thoughtful, added, "So, it's not about rushing to the top just to say you made it."

Sarah wrapped her arm around both kids. "Right. It's about the journey you take together. And sometimes, the best part is the quiet, steady walk, where you learn and grow together."

———

Sexuality is important in our lives, shaping our personal stories and how we relate to each other. At the heart of this is being responsible for us and ensuring our actions reflect our values. This inner guide helps us choose lasting love over just having fun, leading us to relationships based on mutual respect and admiration. Understanding and valuing ourselves and others is critical to our journey through life.

This idea also plays a massive role in the special connection with a future spouse, where being faithful, honest, and supportive lays the groundwork for a meaningful life together. It's about more than just being physically close. It's the coming together of two souls who can share hopes and dreams.

Our choices in sexuality reach beyond just us the couple. The love they share can affect generations to come. The legacy we leave, based on our understanding of love, closeness, and commitment, will shape the world for our children. This bigger picture highlights the impact of our choices on society's future.

In today's fast-paced environment, where instant gratification is the norm and digital connections are continuous, teens face a barrage of conflicting ideas about love and closeness. They require support in navigating these complexities, seeking guidance that transcends mere dos and don'ts. It's about striving for genuine happiness and cherishing the other person as an exceptionally valuable treasure.

The best parts of love aren't about big romantic gestures. They're found in the quiet promises, the steadfast commitment, and our everyday decisions. The most meaningful gift, as I've told my teens, isn't something you can touch. It's the promise of "I waited just for you." This goes beyond temporary excitement to a deep connection.

Drawing from my own family, I remember my dad's stories about the joy and sacredness of waiting for sex until marriage. These weren't outdated lectures but real-life examples of how patience and commitment deepen a bond. These stories remind us that waiting is not just about tradition but a choice that adds so much to a relationship.

While promoting these values, I also spoke to my teens about the reality of marriage, explaining that it has its difficulties. Getting through these challenges requires love, determination, flexibility, and self-control. Though challenging, the reward for this commitment is an enduring connection of trust.

Echoes of Timeless Ties

The Andersons gathered in their living room for a movie night on a cozy Friday evening. As they settled in, Sarah and David saw an opportunity to touch upon a topic they felt was important.

The room, usually abuzz with excitement over which movie to watch, quieted down as Sarah turned to Emma and Max. "Marriage has been a pretty big deal in society," she started, her tone casual yet earnest. "It's more than a legal thing. It's about a partnership that offers support and companionship."

Emma, leaning back with a skeptical look, interjected, "But aren't many people unhappy in their marriages? How does that work with what you're saying?"

David leaned forward, ready to tackle her doubts. "You're right, Emma. Marriage itself isn't a guarantee of happiness. It's about the effort and heart that goes into the relationship."

Max, who had been scrolling through his phone, looked up and wisecracked, "So, it's not like 'get married and live happily ever after,' huh?"

"Exactly," David replied with a smile, acknowledging Max's tone. "It's about building a strong relationship. Research even shows that people in healthy marriages tend to be happier."

Emma, now intrigued, asked, "But how do you make sure it stays healthy? I mean, with what we see around..."

Sarah gently explained, "It's about trust, understanding, and really good communication. And it starts now, with how you manage your relationships and friendships."

"So, we're kind of in training for the future?" Max asked, half-joking but curious.

"In a way, yes," David said. "How you learn to interact and respect others now lays the groundwork for future relationships, including marriage."

Emma nodded. "I heard in our youth group that it's not just about finding the right person. It's about **being** the right person."

"That's a great way to put it," Sarah agreed.

The conversation wound down as the movie began, but the seeds of thought were planted in Emma and Max's minds. Sarah and David exchanged a look of quiet satisfaction, knowing that tonight's discussion was just another step in guiding their teens toward understanding the deeper aspects of relationships and marriage.

———

In today's ever-changing world, the Anderson family's chat reminds us that some fundamental values, like true love, always stay important, no matter how much the setup of families changes from big extended ones to smaller, closer groups. This talk was a chance for Sarah and David to help their teens see that strong, respectful relationships are built on promises and commitment.

Marriage has always been important in communities, being more than just living together. It's about supporting each other emotionally and mentally, and when it's going right, it makes both people feel valued and respected. Even though marriage looks different in various places and times, its goal is to create a special bond that makes life better.

Research has found that married people often lead healthier, happier, and longer lives compared to single folks.[1] Studies also point out that kids from married families tend to do better than those from other setups.[2] The reasons are a bit complex, but it seems like a stable, loving home helps children grow up well-rounded.

Parenting is an art where listening, talking things through, and handling disagreements well are key. These actions not only solve today's issues but also help kids feel valued and connected, setting a foundation for their future.

How parents raise their kids really matters. Working together, being consistent, listening softly, and talking about tough stuff can make family life smoother. Money issues can stress a marriage but tackling them as a team can strengthen the bond.

Life can be complicated, and not every family story includes a happy marriage. Breakups can be hard, but this doesn't take away the opportunity to instruct young people about meaningful relationships. Whether we've been through it ourselves or learned from others, sharing these lessons can guide our kids toward deeper, more fulfilling connections.

Seeds, Wisdom, and a Nurtured Generation

Looking back on my journey as a parent, I've realized the importance of getting teens ready for the commitments of marriage and family life. I often found myself focusing on the what-ifs, trying to protect them from potential problems. In doing this, I now see that I might not have given enough credit to the beauty and value of being patient and waiting. My advice was not just about avoiding risks but also about building emotional depth and a strong connection that grows from waiting with patience for the right person. It was also about becoming the best person possible for others.

I sometimes wish I had found a better balance in my guidance, mixing caution with the benefits of patience. It's important to prepare our kids for challenges, but we should also encourage them to enjoy life's beautiful moments.

Watching my kids in their own families fills me with pride and a bit of humility. They face the usual family difficulties, but their strong family ties, forgiveness, and love stand out. This strength and resilience help them through tough times and keep their relationships strong and loving.

A big part of their strength comes from knowing that life is about more than just individual achievements. It's about the stories we create together. This sense of purpose, deeply connected to our faith, guides them through uncertain times and gives them a solid foundation. This faith-driven purpose adds depth to their lives, enhancing their relationships and helping them connect across generations.

Our grandchildren, with their laughter and energy, show the strength of the connections their parents have built. It's like we planted seeds of wisdom and kindness, and now we're watching them grow into strong trees that protect and nurture the family. This legacy of love and values is evident in the close and caring relationships we see today.

Reflecting on how to nurture true love in teens, I've learned that parents should act more as confident guides than as worried watchers. We're like experienced sailors who respect the sea's unpredictability but trust in our ship's strength. We should believe in our teens' abilities to make smart choices with the proper guidance. This trust is vital to creating an environment where teens feel enlightened to make their own decisions.

Think of parents as expert archers, now handing the bow to their teens. They give them the tools and wisdom they've gathered, then step back to let their teens make their own choices. This trust isn't a step into the unknown but a step back built on a solid foundation.

By adopting this approach, parents avoid overwhelming their teens with fear. Fear can cloud a teen's view, making it hard for them to see their strengths and future. On the other hand, trust and confidence clear the path, helping teens aim confidently at their visions, knowing their parents believe in them.

In this process, parents learn that their fears, though well-meant, can strain a relationship. Teens are sensitive to their parents' feelings and can sense their worries, which might make them doubt themselves. To avoid this, parents should try to embody calm confidence. This doesn't mean ignoring dangers or skipping tough talks. It means having these conversations with a belief in their teen's ability to learn, grow, and choose wisely.

Wings of True Love

In a small, cozy town, nestled between rolling hills and whispering streams, there lived a wise old owl named Oliver. Oliver was known throughout the land for his profound wisdom and understanding of the heart. One day, a young sparrow named Sophie came to him, her wings fluttering with uncertainty.

"Oliver," Sophie began, "I see the world changing around me. The trees seem to whisper of love and companionship, but I'm not sure how to listen. How do I find true love in such a vast forest?"

Oliver looked at Sophie with kind, knowing eyes. "Ah, young one, the journey to true love is much like the flight we take each day. It's not about the speed with which we soar but the grace with which we navigate the winds."

He continued, "Imagine you're flying toward the horizon, eager to explore. Along the way, you'll find many currents. Some will lift you higher, and others might lead you astray. The secret, dear Sophie, is to know your heart just as you know your wings."

Sophie listened intently, her heart beating with hope and curiosity.

"True love," Oliver explained, "is like finding the current that complements your own, where you can glide side by side, sharing the view and the journey. It's built on patience, understanding, and mutual respect, much like the friendships you see in the forest."

Sophie thought about her friends, the playful rabbits, the steady deer, and the bustling bees, all different but living together in harmony.

"But how will I know when I've found it?" she asked.

Oliver smiled warmly. "You'll know, Sophie. True love seems like flying in a warm, gentle breeze. It lifts you, supports you, and brings out the best in you. And remember, it's not just about finding another to fly with but also about being the best version of yourself, ready to share the journey."

Sophie nodded, a sense of calm filling her heart. "Thank you, Oliver. I understand now. It's not about the rush of the wind but the joy of the flight."

With that, Sophie took off, her wings strong and her heart open, ready for the journey ahead. And as she flew, the forest seemed to sing a little sweeter, for within its depths, another soul was learning to navigate the winds of love.

Reflections on Fostering Authentic Connections

As the Andersons delve deep into heart-to-hearts, they're piecing together how the world's rapid changes are reshaping our views on love and closeness. Sarah and David are on a mission, one that's less about following the crowd and more about cultivating a kind of love that's rich with respect and deep connections. They're all about setting the stage for their teens to grasp that true love isn't a "follow-the-leader" game.

This journey? It's all about tapping into the heart's vast ocean. Picture this as an exploration that isn't pushed or prodded. It unfolds on its own, revealing insights into a kind of love that's hard to put into words.

When teens take a moment to just be, to breathe, and let the world around them quiet down, something amazing happens. Their minds, often buzzing like a busy city, start to calm down, and in that calmness, a space opens up. This space is where inner wisdom likes to hang out. It's been there all along, but with the constant go, go, go, it's drowned out.

This inner wisdom is like a wise old friend who knows all your stories, hopes, and dreams. It's that voice that nudges us toward what's good and true. By nurturing a connection with this inner wisdom, teens can discover a love that's not just about them but extends outwards in generous, boundless ways. This wisdom leads to actions that aren't simply good for them but are also good for their friends, family, and the wider community. It's about creating ripples of goodness that start from within and spread out, touching lives and making the world a little brighter.

In a world that often values the fastest, the loudest, and the most, having teens slow down, clear their minds, and connect with their inner wisdom is like handing them a secret map to a treasure trove of goodness. It's a journey worth taking, for the treasure at the end is a life lived with generosity, kindness, and boundless love.

The beauty of hope, love, and companionship is that they're timeless. They're immune to the ticking clock and always priceless. Love is like a beacon of hope and bravery, even when the night is darkest. In today's world, materialism and instant gratification often steal the spotlight. A yearning for an inner moral compass is the answer.

This means living with a heart that's all in for others, downsizing the "me, myself, and I" mindset. It's about putting the spotlight on helping and loving others rather than just focusing on what's good for me alone. Imagine transforming from a solo superstar to a collaborator in the game of life. It's about making "us" and "we" the new cool and sending "me, myself, and I" on a little vacation. It's a vibe where everyone wins because you're sharing the love, not just hoarding it for yourself.

Whether it's conquering trails on a weekend hike or cozying up for a movie night, the Andersons weave in their wisdom on love. It's not just chit-chat. It's preparation for Emma and Max's journey, framing their understanding of marriage and how these pearls of wisdom can uplift society. Through these moments, the Andersons are not just bonding. They're equipping their teens for the future, one heart-to-heart at a time.

The story wraps up with a cute tale about Sophie, who talks to a wise owl named Oliver about finding true love as everything around her keeps changing. Oliver shares some advice about dealing with emotions and the importance of being patient and supporting each other in a relationship. This tale mirrors the lessons the Anderson family talks about, showing Sophie's journey toward finding real, lasting love.

In the next chapter, we'll switch gears a bit. Picture this: You're about to walk through a place where the morning mist makes everything look mysterious. It's all about being careful because you can't see too far ahead. But sometimes, the sun peeks through, and everything gets clearer. That's what we're headed to next in "Journey Through the Mist."

JOURNEY THROUGH THE MIST

Imagine you're walking through a landscape covered in the morning mist, where everything looks cloudy, and the path ahead isn't clear. This is much like being a parent to teens, where steps need to be taken with caution because you're in a fog. Sometimes, though, the sun breaks through, and you can view a path forward, even for a little while. These bright times in parenting are precious, helping to light the way with hope.

These brief, easy-to-miss times can actually change the relationships between parents and teens. They can bring us closer. Think about a simple argument over chores that turns into a meaningful conversation. These moments might seem small, but they're actually impactful.

Imagine a mom and her teen daughter arguing. The air feels heavy with tension. As the day goes on, the daughter opens up about something bothering her. The mom's awareness can spark a quiet conversation. The responses of forgiveness and compassion can clear up all the misunderstandings, and they both feel closer than ever.

Or picture a dad who regrets not being around for his kids enough, feeling guilty as he looks back. When his son comes to him for advice one day, their honest chat can light up their relationship, helping them reconnect. One change in viewpoint can rekindle the bond.

Parents often feel like their efforts to connect with their teens will go unnoticed and have no effect. But it's in these critical moments that we have a chance to really have influence. By hoping for and seizing these chances, we can build lasting bonds of understanding and closeness.

The teen years are full of fluctuations, like constantly shifting scenes. But by keeping an eye out for opportunities and being ready to embrace them, we can build a strong, trusting relationship with teens. This journey, filled with hope, makes every step together a possibility to grow closer and turn disputes into possibilities for deeper interactions.

Hopeful Connections

In life, it's the quiet moments that often sing the loudest, especially when it comes to hope.

For instance, a dad gives a thumbs up to his son's indie playlist, or a mom bravely steps into the world of her teen's latest online adventure. It's not really about the music or the memes. It's about showing trust and hope in our bond with teens.

It's the small stuff that really ties us together. We're talking about everyday moments that might seem minor but are enormous. A shared joke, a hug after a long day, or chilling together can be refreshing. These moments can create a deep attachment that lasts.

Imagine a mom hanging on every word as her teen excitedly talks about a new hobby or a dad slipping an encouraging note into his kid's book. These actions are quiet but powerful, echoing with support, presence, and much love. They play a big part in navigating the teen years, which are packed with social twists, school stress, and the quest to figure out who they are. This steady stream of parental support is like a guiding light for teens as they make their way through the choppy seas of growing up.

This kind of parenting is less about laying down the law and more about being there, valuing those quiet times that knit a tight bond. In these simple moments, the true spirit of parenting shines through, offering teens love and a reminder that they're not alone on their journey. These aren't just fun times. They're the remembrances that turn into stories told over and over again.

Take teaching teens to drive, for instance. It's way more than just learning to operate a car. It's trusting and growing together. Even when our teen is nervous and we're a bit worried, every little win is a reason to celebrate, filling teens and us with pride.

We want to be more than just rule enforcers. Although that's part of parenting, we also want to be teammates and guides for our teens' discovery of who they are. We want to share our wisdom and experiences. And teens? They're looking for someone who acknowledges them and listens. When these needs are met, conversations can bring us closer and lift our relationships to new heights.

Even simple words, like "well done" or a "thank you," can dramatically affect how connected we feel with our teens. It's about feeling seen and appreciated by each other. Doing activities together, like laughing over a funny movie or cooking up a meal in the kitchen, cements our relationships. These moments make our bond not only close but resilient and enduring.

Sometimes, flipping the script and learning something new from our teens effectively mixes things up. It shows mutual respect and teamwork. And when we tackle something bigger, like a community project, it brings a deeper sense of connection and shared purpose.

These activities open the door to real talks about hopes, dreams, and worries. Sharing these personal moments builds trust and understanding. It's like creating a safety net that makes our relationship close and strong enough to weather any storm. These shared moments aren't just nice to have. They're the glue that holds the parent-teen relationship together, paving the way for ties that are deep, uplifting, and enduring.

Navigating the Mist

Parenting teens is like walking through a world that keeps changing. As the familiar signs of their childhood start to fade, we find ourselves trying to make sense of adolescence. Even when things seem foggy, those moments when we suddenly see things clearly can totally change our relationship. Sometimes, we're perfectly coordinated, but other times, we might hit a wrong note. But through it all, we're always there for them, helping them find their way.

Science has shed some light on what teens go through during these years. This research uncovers the transformations happening within the teenage brain, providing a scientific context that can help us approach their behavior with greater patience and empathy.[1] By grounding our parenting in this knowledge, we're better equipped to navigate the misty path of adolescence and guide them toward their fullest potential.

The part of the brain that helps with making decisions, controlling impulses, and handling emotions is still maturing in teens. Studies using brain scans show that the prefrontal cortex keeps developing into its mid-twenties. This development can make teens more likely to take risks as they're drawn to new experiences. It's an important part of their growth, both in their brains and in their social lives.

Then there's puberty, which brings a flood of hormones that affect both their bodies and their brains. These changes can make emotions feel more intense, which helps explain why teens often seem to be on an emotional rollercoaster.

Research also shows that the amygdala, which is deep in the brain and helps process emotions, is more reactive during these years. This means teens can feel things like happiness, anger, or sadness more deeply, which can add to the whirlwind effect.

Teens bring fresh energy into our family life. Their passion can light the way, even when it feels like we're surrounded by fog. Opening up to the new things they love, like a teen introducing jazz into a home that's always been about classical music, can be an adventure we share.

When we hit bumps in the road, like that textbook case where a teen misses curfew, dealing with it through a lens of understanding rather than leaping to judgments can really change the game. Picture this: your teen walks in late, loaded down with whatever went down that night. If we choose to hit the pause button on lecturing and actually listen first, it can kick-start a real talk. This approach doesn't just dodge the whole "us versus them" vibe. It actually pulls us closer together.

Walking through the teen years can be like trying to see through a thick fog early in the day. Imagine that little by little, the fog starts to clear up, showing us the way forward. That's how our adventure with our teens unfolds. It's all about those special shared moments, those deep conversations, and those quiet times when we listen to each other and connect with our gut feelings. These moments are like adding cool filters to our relationship, making it richer and more vibrant. By valuing these times and being all in with empathetic listening and being open, we grow a bond filled with understanding, love, and a deep sense of getting each other.

Hope's Enduring Imprint

In the dynamic and sometimes challenging landscape of parenting teens, the concept of hope emerges as a beacon, guiding both parents and teens through the fog of adolescence. Hope is more than just a wish. It is a potent catalyst, empowering teens to navigate the complexities of growing up with resilience. It encourages them to envision a life filled with endless possibilities and to approach their journey with courage and determination.

The infusion of hope in the parent-teen dynamic can be transformative. It's about a mutual belief in potential, embracing life's changes, and an optimistic forward gaze. This perspective surpasses the value of material wealth or social status. It fosters a sense of meaning and belonging, essential for emotional well-being as teens enter adulthood. Much like finding our way through the morning fog, hope offers clarity, lighting the path forward with promise and anticipation.

Hope's power is evident in how it shapes memories and moments, leaving an indelible mark on our lives. This was exemplified in the last conversation I had with my mother. In her final days, battling the haze of Alzheimer's, her memory of faces and names had nearly faded away. Yet, in one of our last interactions, a week before she passed, I had a sentimental experience.

During a FaceTime call facilitated by my brother, I saw my mother's eyes. They were barely open but flickering with a faint spark of recognition. She couldn't speak, yet her attempt to reach out through the screen spoke volumes. Her hand, frail and trembling, covered the camera, plunging the screen into darkness. In that darkness, a flood of memories washed over me. I remembered her nurturing care, her radiant warmth, the joy in her eyes, and the countless times she held me close. That simple gesture captured the entirety of our life together.

That was the last time I saw her, the final conversation we

shared. It stood as a testament to the enduring power of love. It's a bond that remained strong and unbreakable, even as memory and recognition faded. This memory is a treasure I hold dear. Love transcends the most challenging circumstances. It's a tribute to the beautiful soul she was and the everlasting impact she made on my heart.

In this story, just as in the journey of parenting teens, the essence of hope and the power of enduring love are present. The ultimate goal of the Inner Connection Quest is not just to manage the teen years but to forge a relationship rich in love and hope, leaving a lasting imprint on both parents and teens. Through the mist of adolescence, hope acts as our guiding light, encouraging us to listen softly, come closer, and build a bridge to a future marked by understanding and deep connection.

Faith Over Fear

Parenting through the teen years often seemed like wandering through a misty forest at dawn. Initially, I approached it like a hiker set on a morning trek, determined and earnest, believing my resolve would somehow disperse the fog for my son. However, this method often felt like we were both navigating through a thick fog, making our journey together more challenging.

The turning point came unexpectedly at a family camp workshop amidst the serene backdrop of a fog-laden morning. A fellow camper shared an insight that pierced through the mist: "When we are afraid, we lose heart." These words struck a chord within me, even though I couldn't quite grasp their full depth at the moment. Yet, they sowed a seed of transformation in my approach.

Inspired by this experience, I chose to let go of my restrictive beliefs. I vividly recall the conversation with my 19-year-old son, where I openly expressed my trust in him and affirmed my unconditional support. This marked a departure from my usual instinct to guide and direct his steps. I acknowledged his capacity to navigate his own path, effectively handing him the compass in the mist.

This shift was deeply rooted in hope and love. By opting to trust and support him, I was not only showing confidence in his decisions but also nurturing our relationship with a love that knows no conditions. It was an acknowledgment that love and hope are like beams of light that can guide us through the fog, allowing us to journey side by side, each on our individual paths, yet connected by an unspoken understanding and mutual respect.

The results were better than I had anticipated. My son flourished with this newfound freedom. He made thoughtful decisions, reflecting a maturity that surprised and delighted me. One evening, he shared how much he appreciated this change in my approach. We both discovered a deeper connection and freedom in this shift from control to trust and fear to faith.

Guided by an Inner Compass

Each of us has an internal navigation system, an intrinsic compass that guides our decisions. This system, often unnoticeable, operates deep within us. Tuning into this inner guidance can transform how we deal with foggy circumstances. Our decision-making process mirrors how in tune we are with our inner guide, our gut feelings, and the wisdom that life offers us.

Consider the agonizing episode involving my grandson, who was only two years old when he suffered burns due to boiling water his mother accidentally spilled. In a situation that would typically send any parent into a spiral of panic and anxiety, she displayed extraordinary composure. Rather than succumbing to distress, she was surprisingly serene, even expressing concern for my safety over the wet floor as I hurried to help. This calmness in the face of a crisis was pivotal when the situation escalated, necessitating my grandson's airlift to a specialized children's hospital.

In most emergencies, parents' strong emotions usually stop them from being allowed to fly with their child, as they might be too upset for the trip. But my daughter-in-law was different. Her calmness and clarity allowed her to stay with her son during the critical helicopter ride. This wasn't something she planned. It was her natural reaction. It shows how our inner sense can guide us in surprising ways, giving us strength and clear thinking when we need it most.

However, the path isn't always straightforward. Sometimes, we act against our better judgment, silencing that soft, guiding whisper within. Reflecting on my experience as a young adult, I once had a chance to fly from California to New York for just three days. Despite not living at home, the thought of informing my parents crossed my mind. I chose to proceed, disregarding that inner voice, thinking the brief absence wouldn't be noticed and I'd share my adventures upon return.

Extending my stay in New York, I found myself at a crossroads, similar to navigating a car through the thick mist of an early morning drive. The decision to change my return ticket brought a dense cloud over my thoughts. The idea of informing my parents about my prolonged stay seemed as daunting as driving with limited visibility. At that moment, the emotional fog was too thick. Confronting the situation felt beyond my capabilities. My choice to stay longer was swept up in a flurry of activities, leaving me in a haze, unable to clear the mist enough to communicate my new circumstances to my parents. This detour from my initial plan brought with it a discomfort, a silent alarm within, hinting that I had veered off the course set by my inner compass.

After a couple of weeks, I received an urgent message from my mother asking me to call her. Through the grapevine, she found out. I immediately called her and had to face the hurt and disappointment. I regretted that decision. Years later, I brought it up again; she had already forgotten about it. That's the heart of forgiveness.

The experience of regret, insecurity, and the endless "what ifs" that follow a decision are all too familiar aspects of the human condition. They highlight our sometimes problematic relationship with decision-making, where our choice can overshadow our inner wisdom. Mistakes are part of our journey. There are moments when we misinterpret our inner compass. We can look at these times not as signs of failure but as opportunities for growth and learning.

Our capacity to make decisions is intricately linked to our state of mind. When fear and anxiety cloud our thoughts, like a snow globe shaken, our imagination runs wild, often leading us astray. In these moments, we can remember we are part of a more extensive, intelligent system that seeks to guide us. By acknowledging this connection, our mind becomes a receptive vessel for insight, open to the guidance and fresh perspectives offered by this intelligence of life. We need to listen softly.

Being open to innovative ideas means trusting ourselves and believing we can find and understand the answers we're looking for. It's about actively seeking knowledge and believing in the idea that "if you ask, you'll get an answer." We're reminded that help and advice are always around, even when we're unsure of ourselves.

There's still something to learn when we mess up or face a dead end. Every mistake teaches us something important, setting us up for what comes next. The lessons we learn from our slip-ups are valuable, preparing us with knowledge for whatever we face down the road.

Think about walking across a simple wooden plank. When it's on the ground, it's no big deal to walk across. But if you raise that plank high up, suddenly it seems scary and hard to cross. This change shows how stress affects us. Things that are typically easy can seem really hard when we're stressed out.

This applies to making decisions, too. Stress can cloud our thinking, making choices feel much more complicated. The key is to take a moment to calm down and slow down our thoughts. This can make the situation seem less stressful, like bringing the plank back down to the ground, making it easier to walk across. By doing this, we start to see challenges not just as problems but as chances to grow and learn.

When we're true to our deepest selves, we connect with more honesty, kindness, and openness toward others. At the heart of the Inner Connection Quest is the gentle art of tuning into our inner voice. This practice strengthens our relationship with ourselves, enriching the quality of our interactions.

Finding Clarity in the Fog

Walking through the teen years is like moving through a foggy scene at dawn, where it's hard to see the path ahead, but sometimes, light breaks through. These bright spots, like finding common ground after a spat over chores or laughing together at a private joke, really matter. They don't just light up our way but also bring us closer to our teens, turning daily challenges into chances for growth and connection. This is where our Inner Connection Quest kicks off, aiming to build a deeper, more understanding relationship with teens based on trust and hope.

We sometimes need clarification on whether our attempts to connect with teens are getting through. But it's often the trivial things, the moments that might seem small, that have the most significant impact. By looking for these chances to connect, we set the stage for a bond built on talking openly, sharing experiences, and appreciating each other.

Hopefully, we've seen glimpses of clarity as we've tried to decipher the secret language of eye rolls and one-word responses. Now, imagine channeling that clarity into actions that bring us closer to our teens and enlighten them to make their mark on the world.

In PART III - MAKING A DIFFERENCE, we're diving head-first into the art of turning everyday moments into opportunities for growth. It's not just about making an impact on the world. It's about igniting a spark within teens, showing them the power of their actions, and watching that flame turn into a wildfire of positive change. So, buckle up and prepare for an inspiring ride as we discover how to amplify our creative nature and meaning in life.

PART THREE

MAKING A DIFFERENCE

Getting involved in causes we care about can be fulfilling. The Inner Connection Quest is a journey that helps us grow by gently tuning into our creativity and finding ways to make a difference. This journey shows us how valuable we are and helps us find meaningful ways to contribute. It's a path of discovery that teaches us how to make a positive impact in ways that really matter to us.

ANCHORED IN UNDERCURRENTS

THE AROMA OF FRESHLY BREWED COFFEE DRIFTED THROUGH the air, mingling with the low hum of conversations. In New York City's bustling streets, "Undercurrents" was an oasis of warmth and calm. The comfortable wooden chairs and the soft playing of old jazz music made this coffee shop a sanctuary. It was a perfect hideaway for anyone wanting to take a break from the city's fast pace.

Sarah, always in formal suits and heels, worked intensely on her laptop in the relaxed café. Her focused demeanor showed the stress of her corporate job. But on Wednesdays, her expression softened. She would order two extra coffees along with her latte and leave them at a table near the entrance. Tom and Lisa, dressed in worn clothes, would quietly enter and light up at the sight of the coffee. They never spoke to Sarah, but their grateful looks said everything.

When others asked about the extra coffee, Sarah would smile and change the topic. She kept her help discreetly, respecting Tom and Lisa's dignity. Unlike others who often seek recognition for virtuous deeds, Sarah's quiet actions showed her deep compassion. She didn't want any praise, just the happiness that comes from helping others.

Leo's glasses glistened in a corner behind his book. His wrinkled fingers turned the pages with a reverence only old age and wisdom could bring. But what intrigued others most were the moments he paused, looking up, observing, and then scribbling fervently in his worn-out leather journal. His entries weren't just musings but descriptions of life unfolding around him. Whether it was the young couple sharing a secretive smile, the anxious writer biting her pen, or the child's wonder at the whipped cream on his cocoa, Leo captured them. These stories, he believed, were his gift to future generations.

Many perceived Leo as a solitary soul. Little did they know he was collecting stories of love and altruism he saw in the coffee shop. Leo wasn't a bestselling author or a journalist; he was a retired schoolteacher. His aim was to create a collection of tales for his grandchildren, hoping to instill in them the values of love and self-lessness.

Behind the counter, Mia moved gracefully, making even the mundane act of pouring coffee seem like an elegant dance. Her infectious laughter made the gloomiest of days brighter. But it was her attentiveness that endeared her to all. She knew more than just their coffee preferences. She remembered their stories. When Mr. Rodriguez, a regular, seemed downcast one day, Mia surprised him with his favorite almond biscotti and a simple note: "For brighter days ahead." It was her way of showing she cared without saying anything.

As days turned into weeks, regular patrons began to notice Mia's subtle acts. When asked about it, Mia would wink and say, "Just a little sprinkle of magic for the day." She never boasted about these gestures or saw them as anything extraordinary. For Mia, it was her way of weaving warmth into the fabric of everyday life. This was a testament to the belief that sometimes, the smallest gestures hold the deepest meanings.

"Undercurrents" was like a river where countless lives and tales flowed together. Interactions were like streams feeding into this ever-growing waterway. It served as a reminder that beneath the daily grind and the masks we wear, there's this powerful current of love, kindness, and awesome human vibes. In this haven, life wasn't merely experienced. It was deeply valued and treasured.

Depths of Inner Value

It's easy to dismiss the bustling world of teens as a myriad of changing friendships, new interests, and, of course, the omnipresent technology. The societal narrative often paints a picture of teens as being distracted, disengaged, or simply rebellious. But just as with the patrons of "Undercurrents," looking beyond the surface often reveals an ocean of depth, emotion, and genuine affection.

Teenagers may not always publicly display their genuine acts of love and concern. The support they provide to a struggling friend, their concern for a sibling, or their voluntary community service often remain unseen. Parents might only see the tip of the iceberg, like the grades or the occasional defiance, but beneath that usually lies a reservoir of compassion and growing maturity.

Similarly, as Mia subtly adjusted her actions based on her understanding of her customers, teens, too, have an innate ability to tune into the emotions of those around them. Their endless hours of chatter, texts, or video calls are often their way of connecting and supporting each other. While parents might see it as a mere distraction, it could be their way of adding value to someone's day or helping a friend navigate through a challenging phase.

Leo's chronicling of the world around him is reminiscent of a teen's journey of self-discovery. They are constantly observing, internalizing, and learning. Their diaries, blogs, or even social media posts can be their way of making sense of the world, capturing moments of love, altruism, or simply the beauty of everyday life.

We can probe deeper, beyond the surface of grades, hobbies, or even mood swings of teens. Engaging in open conversations, displaying genuine interest in their daily activities, and, most importantly, acknowledging and appreciating their small acts of kindness and compassion can go a long way in helping teens recognize and cherish their inner value.

In a world where teens are often boxed into stereotypes, parents can guide them to recognize and celebrate the undercurrents of genuine emotion and love that define their journey. It's about seeing beyond the obvious, understanding their silent struggles, and championing the unseen acts that capture their growth and inner value.

Think of it like going on a deep-sea dive, way past the glitzy surface where all the trophies and big moments sparkle. What you'd find is the real deal. It's the quiet but sincere heart of who we really are. So, when we're figuring ourselves out or checking someone else out, we can go deeper into the beliefs and values that are the real MVPs behind the choices we make and the dreams we're sprinting after. It's not just about the flashy stuff we can see. It's about what fires us up inside to go after what really counts.

True value lies deep down. It's an idea that might get lost in the glitz of success but lights the way to a life of impact and purpose. Life is a vast network of crossing paths and intertwining stories, held together not by loud victories or glaring setbacks but by the strong, silent core within each of us.

Imagine a journey not aimed at a specific endpoint but at peeling back the layers of self to reveal TRUE LOVE. At the start, you find self-worth, the quiet recognition that our value isn't only about the difficulties we face but stands firm against the storms of judgment.

Go a little further, and authenticity emerges. Being true to our feelings and thoughts is a bold move. It's about embracing the natural, unpolished self that each of us carries. Then, there's the compass of moral integrity, guiding us to do what's right, even when shortcuts are tempting. It's our silent protector, keeping us true to our beliefs.

Understanding others is also key on this path. Empathy lets us connect with the wide array of feelings others go through, building bridges in a divided world. Challenges might pop up, but resilience shines through, reminding us of our inner strength and value.

In the cozy corners of 'Undercurrents,' amidst the scent of coffee and background chatter, we see the power of recognizing our inner wealth. It's the silent recognition of our essence and the impact of our actions that truly makes a difference. While the outside world may chase after grand displays, inside this haven, the quiet moments and the appreciation of heart that resonate the loudest.

Anchored in Value

Imagine a ship enduring a stormy sea. The giant waves and gusty winds threaten to throw it off course. However, beneath its deck lies the anchor, stabilizing the vessel and ensuring it doesn't drift astray. When challenges often appear as those unpredictable storms, one's inner connection plays a similar anchoring role.

Resilience is about understanding why one should. It's here that the power of recognizing inherent worth shines brightly. In the face of setbacks, instead of being swayed by the storms of doubt or external judgments, individuals grounded in their inherent ideals find the strength to persevere. This isn't a stubborn defiance of challenges but a deep-rooted understanding that one's essence transcends the immediate hurdles.

As we go through life, filled with its tales of triumphs and tribulations, it's crucial to remember that inner wisdom is more than just a concept. It's the very foundation of our being. This quiet voice offers counsel when crossroads appear. The gentle nudge steers us toward paths aligned with TRUE LOVE. It offers direction and purpose, ensuring the journey is meaningful, no matter how winding.

When our worth feels quantified by titles or social media followers, it's time to remember this silent, steadfast compass within. Beyond the societal roles and labels, this deep sense of inner value carves out a life of authenticity and fulfillment beyond the fleeting applause. It's not just about navigating the challenges. It's about transforming them into stepping stones, leading to a life that genuinely has influence.

Sarah, the Wall Street executive, seems to float atop the corporate hierarchy, but even she faces her share of wild storms. Remember those Wednesdays when she'd order two extra cups of coffee? They weren't just for Tom and Lisa. They were her anchor amidst a week that might have been burdened with professional challenges. Her recognition of her inner worth enabled her to see beyond her immediate challenges, offering warmth in the face of cold corporate winds.

Then there's Leo, the observer. One might wonder why he writes about the lives of café customers. But delve deeper, and you'll realize that there were moments of self-doubt for every story, questioning the purpose of his writings. Yet, anchored in his inherent value, he saw beyond the immediate challenges, realizing that his tales were not just stories but legacies.

Mia, the barista, might seem to have the simplest job, but behind her sunny smile lie her battles. Each time a customer was less than kind or when the weight of her personal challenges threatened to bring her down, her inner wisdom allowed her to respond with poise and patience. She transformed potential conflicts into moments of connection and care.

Challenges are as certain as the dawn. It's a silent song of perception that provides rhythm and tone. The patrons of 'Undercurrents,' each in their unique way, embody this. They don't just face challenges. They draw strength from their inner connection and have an influence on the lives of those they touch.

This cozy coffee shop, called Undercurrents, became the stage for something amazing. It shows us how doing trivial things with a lot of heart can make life richer and more meaningful.

This is what Viktor Frankl refers to as logotherapy, a fancy term that says finding meaning in life is super important.[1] In this story, whether it's through small acts of kindness, jotting down thoughts, or just making someone's day a little brighter, the characters are all about making each moment count.

"Undercurrents" shows us that life is about the everyday moments and the choices we make to be kind, to connect with others, and to face challenges head-on. For parents and teens alike, this story is a reminder that the trivial things can make a substantial difference. It's about finding joy and purpose in the daily grind, one cup of coffee, one smile, one kind act at a time.

Finding Flow in Teen Turmoil

Picture the Garden of Eden, right out of the Bible, where everything was mellow until Adam and Eve decided to snack on the one thing they were told to avoid. Suddenly, they're feeling all exposed and freaking out among the foliage. When God asks them, "Where are you?" It's not just about their hide-and-seek skills. This moment, when Eden's peace was shattered, is relatable. It's like when we're trying to manage our own crazy thoughts and feelings, feeling all lost and overwhelmed.

God's question wasn't about their GPS coordinates but was digging into their emotional and spiritual GPS. That's like us when we're lost in our headspace, our thoughts swirling around like a snow globe that's been given a good shake. Inside, what was once a mellow scene turns into a blizzard of confusion, making it tough to see where we're headed.

Ever feel like you're not measuring up or you're on your own little island? Those thoughts can hit like a storm, building walls between us and the world. Stuck in this whirlwind of doubts and downers, we all crave change. But just like any storm, these rough patches pass.

Eventually, our thoughts settle, the snowflakes of our minds find peace, and everything's clear again. In that quiet, magic happens.

After the storm in our minds calms down, we find this extraordinary moment of listening softly. It's like finding wisdom that had been hidden between our chaotic thoughts. On these mellow occasions, when the mind is not all over the place, we connect with something more significant. Call it God, the universe, some major life force, or whatever, but that connection brings a real-ness and confidence that's hard to see when we're in the middle of a mental tornado.

In these clear-headed times, ideas and solutions flow. It's like our inner GPS is set to "intuition," guiding us through even the most challenging situations. This clarity and insight show how helpful it can be to just pause and let our minds take a breather, revealing the wisdom that's been inside us all along.

That ancient question, "Where are you?" is our own personal shout-out, reminding us that beneath our everyday hustle, there's a deeper, more epic part of us waiting to be explored.

Sarah, with her low-key goodness, Leo, with his storytelling, and Mia, with her soft heart, show us how deep diving beyond the surface can totally change the game. Like an anchor in stormy waters, tapping into our inner strength lets us face life's dramas without losing ourselves. Their journeys are all about the power and resilience we unlock by getting real with who we are.

Watching teens can sometimes be like watching them in their

own version of Eden. As they figure out their place in the world, they might pull a classic Adam and Eve, hiding out and wrestling with big-time emotions and identity quests.

Just like back in the day, parents could ask their teens, "Where are you?" It's not to grill them but as an invite to chat. It can help us ride out the adolescent storm together. It's a way for parents to get the inside scoop on their teen's evolving world.

In the café of life, we get a front-row seat to teens' journey. They're sorting out who they are, where they fit in, and learning more about what drives them. Beyond all the tech and mood swings, every teen is on an Inner Connection Quest to discover what really lights them up and who they're meant to be.

Harmony Beyond Self

Envision being in a state of tranquility, allowing our thoughts to dissolve until we reach a serene place deep within, where our mind finds its balance. It's like stumbling upon the perfect soundtrack that resonates with our soul. If we find this tranquility, our senses will be heightened, as if we've shifted from standard definition to high resolution. We can clear away all distractions and focus our awareness. Suddenly, we're not just an individual. We're engaging in a broader dialogue with the universe.

Have you spent much time in nature? It's the ultimate natural detox for our mind. The sound of rustling leaves, the whispers of the wind, and the symphony of frogs by the pond are nature's orchestra for us. By emptying our minds and absorbing nature in its entirety, we dissolve the barrier between ourselves and the natural world. We experience joy. Suddenly, nature doesn't just surround us. We become one with it.

From childhood, I've appreciated nature and the harmony in everything, from the songs of pine trees to the choruses of insects. In nature, everything functions in a perfectly coordinated manner, without any element seeking attention or being neglected. It has been a source of comfort and strength throughout my life, providing solace in challenging times and lifting me up in moments of despair.

Unfortunately, many young people today grow up in urban environments, detached from this natural connection. This disconnection is regrettable because forming a bond with nature is as crucial as academic achievements. Accumulating knowledge without experiencing the world's natural rhythm is like navigating life without fully engaging one's senses. One of my fondest memories was getting to the top of a mountain and overlooking the scenery. The shimmer of the water, the crispness of the breeze, the sun's gentle embrace, the earthy perfume of the redwood trees, and the serene silence wrapped around me like a hug filled with love.

The power of love and deep-seated wisdom dwells within each of us. Love is the most potent force in the universe.

The secret handshakes of connecting with the world around us are noticing such things as the different tunes played by spring and autumn rain or appreciating the roadside dandelion's pop of yellow. Loving nature is like being in tune with the people in our life. Without this love, we miss the core of what it means to be alive. Everything in the universe, no matter how small or insignificant, like a grain of sand, to something as complex as human life, contributes to the grand narrative of the cosmos. Starting to love nature kicks off a journey of understanding and falling head over heels for the magnificence of everything that exists.

To deepen our ability to love others, we can begin by cultivating self-awareness and empathy. Just as we tune into the subtle notes of nature and its seasons, we can learn to attune ourselves to the feelings and needs of those around us. This process starts with softly listening to the stories, dreams, and concerns of others without judgment or the intent to reply immediately. It's about understanding their perspective, even if it differs from ours.

Expressing gratitude plays a crucial role in loving others more deeply. Just like the dandelion, often overlooked yet resilient and full of life, we can appreciate the people in our lives for their unique qualities and the enduring moments they share with us. This acknowledgment can be verbal, through acts of kindness, or even through a simple, heartfelt gesture. It signals to others that they are valued and seen.

Practicing forgiveness is another vital step toward loving others more. Holding onto grievances is like refusing to acknowledge the changing seasons. It prevents us from moving forward and experiencing new growth. Forgiveness does not mean excusing harmful behavior. It's about releasing the burden of resentment so we can continue to love and interact with others from a place of peace and heart.

Last but not least, committing to acts of kindness and generosity can significantly enhance our ability to love others. These acts, whether big or small, can transform not just the lives of the recipients but our own lives as well. By giving without the expectation of receiving anything in return, we tap into a bottomless well of love. It's a reminder that, like the interconnectedness of all things in nature, our well-being is tied to the well-being of those around us.

Embracing these steps invites us to extend love more freely and openly, mirroring the boundless love we witness in the natural world. We can contribute to a more compassionate and loving world by practicing empathy, gratitude, forgiveness, and kindness.

Wrapping up this chapter, let's soak in the wisdom "Undercurrents" shares. It highlights the journey to find who we are and make a mark on the world. It's paved with moments of quiet understanding, acts of kindness that resonate beyond the immediate, and an unwavering faith in our own worth. This exploration of life beneath the surface is more than words on a page. It encourages us to look deeper and support teens in their quest for identity and purpose.

Next up is "Dylan's Digital Diary." As Dylan seeks out genuine connections, his story invites us to think about our own digital habits. See how Dylan's changes not just his life, but also inspires others to reconnect with the world around them.

DIGITAL DIARY OF DYLAN

Dylan lived in Metroville, a city pulsating with the rhythms of technology. At 17, his face, though young, was recognized by many, thanks to his popular YouTube channel, streaming right from the devices of thousands of subscribers. The latest tech gadget? Dylan was the go-to. Each video highlighted not just the sleekest phones or the most advanced smartwatches but also a teen who, to the world, seemed to have cracked the code to modern-day success. But behind the pixelated facade of likes and comments lay a more sincere quest, an itch that the newest gadgets couldn't scratch.

As the amber sun of an autumn evening descended over Metroville, Dylan sat down with the day's delivery of the latest, much-anticipated tech gadget. As he began the ritual of unboxing, peeling away layers of sleek packaging, and feeling the cool touch of the device, an unexpected weight settled in his heart.

There, amidst the gleam of his new possession and the gentle rustling of discarded packaging, Dylan's thoughts drifted. A silence enveloped him, muting the distant sounds of Metroville's bustling streets below. The very device that was supposed to amplify his digital existence instead made him think.

"Is this it?" he pondered, holding the gadget to the dimming light. "When all's said and done, will my worth, my legacy, be reduced to just likes, comments, and shares?"

Dylan decided to try something bold. What about "Offline October," a month without any digital distractions? He grabbed a leather-bound journal, a gift from his grandmother he'd never used before. The empty pages called out to him. Dylan was ready to swap the shine of screens for the enduring flow of ink on paper, recording life as it's truly lived, not just as it's shown online.

———

As the weeks went by, Dylan's exploration of the real world marked a change in him. The constant sounding of notifications faded away, replaced by the calming memory of his grandmother sharing stories from her past. These stories, full of resilience and courage, connected Dylan to a world where people bonded over shared experiences and genuine laughter.

On one quiet afternoon walk, Dylan was drawn to the sound of a piano coming from the local community center's dance studio. Peering through the glass, he saw Ava moving with elegance, teaching children how to dance. Her every move conveyed a sense of freedom. Ava's world was vibrant and full of life, echoing with children's laughter, the swish of her skirt, and the heartfelt rhythm of the music.

Moved by these experiences, Dylan felt a strong urge to share his journey. He turned to the journal his grandmother had given him and began writing. What he wrote down was "What Really Matters?" a reflection that soon resonated with teens across the globe. They shared their stories of stepping away from the digital blur to discover the warmth of real-life connections.

Parents, who had been watching their teens grow more attached to screens, saw Dylan's story as a ray of hope. His experience sparked a movement in Metroville, the "Offline Challenge." This wasn't just a trend but a wake-up call for the youth to rediscover the beauty of simple life experiences.

In his writings, Dylan began to weave together technology and life's important lessons, encouraging his followers to take time away from their electronics to enjoy the world's true wonders. He reminded them that the real beauty of life lies in timeless human stories and the connections we forge with each other.

Searching for Meaning

Metroville is a small version of the big challenges we all face today. Here, we meet Dylan, a teen who has everything he could want in terms of things, but he's still asking questions about what life really means.

The idea of what's valuable in life is really tied to why we think we're here. When we're not sure what our vision or direction is, it feels like the ground under us starts to shake. All the experiences we could have seem less interesting, and we start feeling like something's missing.

Philosophers, including Kant, have pondered this subject deeply. Kant believed that our actions gain value when we do what's right simply because it is the right thing to do.[1] However, this raises a question. If our actions are driven solely by duty, without a larger purpose, can we truly feel a sense of meaning?

These questions about why we're here and what makes life valuable aren't just for thinking about alone. They're tied to what we all sense. Religions have tried to answer these questions, usually talking about our personal journey. Buddhism, for example, discusses growing on the inside and being kind, but it doesn't always give clear advice for the bigger picture of how society works.

Christianity tells us to love Jesus and each other, focusing on how we function as individuals. But sometimes, it's hard to find advice for the tricky problems in our larger, connected world. The fact that groups like the hippies have popped up shows that a lot of people are looking for meaning and value that goes beyond the usual answers.

Even still, we should carefully listen to the core of whatever religion we belong to or the spirituality we practice. Hope and faith are awe inspiring. With clarity of thought comes wisdom. We can't be taught wisdom. It has to be experienced from within. If we are filled with wonder, it means that something in our deepest consciousness has been touched.

Even areas like politics and money, which might seem really different from these deep questions, are actually influenced by them. The way our society is set up shows what we all value.

So, if we take a moment to think about it, to understand what really matters today, we need to search for a deeper reason behind everything. This broader goal, beyond just our personal views, can help us all figure out what's important in a world that's both incredibly connected and yet feels quite divided. At the heart of everything, there's a powerful energy that's the source of all life. Wisdom is already inside each of us, waiting to be discovered. The challenge lies in connecting to that larger purpose.

Beyond the Digital Veil

Metroville, in its afternoon brilliance, shimmered under the warm sun, highlighting the vibrant colors of busy sidewalk cafes. The city's rhythm, a blend of midday bustle and laid-back lunchtime gatherings, was unmistakable. Children's laughter, the distant murmur of conversations, and the melodies from a street musician's guitar filled the air.

On this particular afternoon, Dylan walked the streets with a renewed sense of wonder. The constant companionship of his earbuds, once feeding him an unending stream of digital tunes, was now gone. He was fully immersed with every step synchronizing with Metroville's real-time heartbeat.

Dylan's path led him to an art alley, a hidden gem of Metroville. He paused, observing a local artist breathing life onto a blank canvas. The evolving art piece, an abstract blend of hues, reminded Dylan of the untapped potential and raw creativity within everyone, waiting to be discovered and expressed.

As he ventured further, he stumbled upon a community kitchen. Here, the aroma of hearty soup merged with the laughter of its volunteers. Dylan, drawn in, found himself dishing out warm meals alongside strangers. There were no cameras, no digital records, just a joyful act of service. The smiles of gratitude he received were more rewarding than any online success.

The next day, as the sun began its gentle descent over Metroville, Dylan found himself wandering the streets again. The early evening air was filled with the familiar sounds of the city. It featured the distant hum of traffic, laughter from nearby cafes, and the chirping of birds returning to their nests.

Suddenly, a different kind of sound stood out. The soft, rhythmic beats of a drum pulled him like a magnet. Intrigued, he followed the sound; a particular figure stood out to Dylan among the familiar sights and sounds. It was Ava, whom he recognized from the dance studio. There she was, a vision of grace and elegance, dancing freely. The children encircling her lit up with the pure delight of the moment.

Leaps defied gravity, and the steps resonated with the beat of the drum, creating a mesmerizing harmony. Unable to resist, the children joined in, trying to imitate her moves. Their laughter, innocent attempts at mimicking her, and sheer joy added a magical charm to the scene. Some were naturals, flowing with the rhythm, while others stumbled, earning chuckles and encouragement from their peers.

Dylan viewed the scene from the sidelines. A smile slowly formed. To him, this wasn't just a dance. Through her performance, Ava instilled in these young souls an appreciation for tradition, beauty, and the simple joys of life. Dylan realized then, more than ever, that moments like these, raw, genuine, and bursting with life, were the true nature of what it meant to be alive.

With each day, Dylan's perspective shifted. The city beckoned him to uncover its lesser-known treasures. One early evening, his attention was drawn to a quaint bookstore. Its wooden exterior was subtly lit by pastel lights, providing a soft contrast to the neon glows nearby.

Inside, amidst stacks of classic novels and historical narratives, was an elderly couple. Elias, with silver hair neatly combed back, and his wife, graceful with lines of wisdom etched on her face, radiated contentment. Their discussions painted vivid imagery of an era when authenticity was the norm, not the exception.

"The advancements today," Elias said, with a gentle sigh, "are great. But sometimes, I feel they overshadow the heartfelt simplicities we grew up with."

His wife, softly touching the spine of a faded book, responded, "It's true. We can reach out to the world with a tap, but there's a depth of connection we sometimes miss."

Drawn into their world, Dylan shared, "I felt that too. We spend so much time on our devices that we risk missing life's special moments."

In that warm, inviting nook of Metroville, their shared reflections gave a gentle nudge to the soul. It was an invitation to embrace the present. As they parted ways, the air carried a silent promise to cherish the warmth of human connection. This encounter, a fleeting moment in time, left an indelible mark, a gentle reminder that in our quest for progress, we shouldn't lose sight of the simple joys that enrich life.

Inner Value in Metroville

Dylan stood at Metroville's central plaza, the very place where, not so long ago, he had been captivated by the vibrant pulse of life. But today, his presence wasn't that of an observer.

Around him, a crowd had gathered for a day of service. Armed with paintbrushes, teens were reviving a once-neglected corner of Metroville, turning gray walls into canvases bursting with life. Families, from toddlers to grandparents, planted trees, each one a testament to hope, growth, and natural beauty.

Dylan's journey wasn't just about personal growth. It sparked a community awakening. His quest for inner value, independent of digital validation, resonated with countless others. Families discovered joy in their projects, from tending community gardens to volunteering at local food banks. Together, they found fulfillment in genuine, unfiltered real-life experiences.

Amidst the hum of activities, a soft melody floated through the air. A group of teens, with guitars and makeshift drums, played a tune that expressed the spirit of Metroville's transformation. The lyrics spoke of truth, beauty, goodness, and finding inner value.

Elias, with his wife by his side, approached Dylan. "Look at what you've sparked," he mused, his eyes reflecting pride. "You've reminded Metroville that there's an unmatched beauty in authentic interactions and lending a hand."

Dylan replied, "I found what really matters."

Elias chuckled, "And in doing so, young man, you've illuminated a path for many."

The plaza buzzed with vibrant energy as the day faded with a fusion of laughter, gratitude, art, and shared stories. Once lost in the vastness of the digital realm, Dylan had found his purpose. In doing so, he had led Metroville to rediscover its soul.

———

Everyone has their personal expression of heart, from tech-smart teens like Dylan to wise elders like Elias. This value isn't about how many followers we have online or getting applause from others. It's something very personal, shaped by our experiences, beliefs, dreams, and our human spirit.

So, how do we really understand this unique value? One way is through helping others. When we do things for people, show understanding, and connect, we start to see parts of ourselves we didn't know were there. Helping can uncover what we're enthusiastic about and the impact we can have.

Helping others also brings people together. Their differences fade away when young and old work together, whether on community projects or just sharing stories. Instead, a strong bond forms, built on shared experiences and respect. This shows us that even though our stories might be different, listening softly for truth, beauty, and goodness has the same benefit for everyone.

Guiding Teens: The FROGS Dance

Imagine a dance with parents and teens. Sometimes the steps are familiar. Other times, teens might lead us into an unexpected rhythm. To move in harmony, our mind can be serene and free of judgment or anxiety. This is dancing with our heart, letting trust and empathy guide each step rather than following a predetermined routine.

By embracing FROGS—Flexibility, Rapport, Outcome,

Grounding, and Simple Conversations—we're given a map that transforms parenting into a heartfelt approach for nurturing teens' success. It's through this plan we discover the steps to foster a stronger bond and support teens on their journey.

Being flexible means that we keep up with teens' changing world, making sure we're always there in the right way. Rapport is about building a deep connection, so our teens feel listened to and seen. Aiming for good outcomes helps them see their own value and what they're good at. Speaking from a place of grounded knowledge and honesty gives our teen confidence. Simple conversations are those honest talks where they can share freely.

This approach is about making our relationship with teens stronger. It helps us show them how much they matter as we go through these endearing years together.

Listening to teens means hearing not just their words but also the feelings and silent messages they're sending. This helps us catch what they're really saying, including their hopes and dreams.

Consider the metaphor of a girl chasing butterflies. In a sunny garden full of whispering leaves and colorful flowers, there was a girl with a big dream. She wanted to catch butterflies. She ran around with a net, trying her best to catch them, but the butterflies always managed to stay just out of reach. They danced in the air, free and swift, always flying too high or darting too fast.

After many tries, the girl felt tired and a little sad. She sat down on the soft grass, putting her net beside her, and took a deep breath. She looked around at the beautiful garden and began to enjoy the peace and quiet. She wasn't running or jumping anymore. She was sitting there, calm and still.

Something remarkable happened then. The butterflies, which seemed to stay away when she chased them, started to get closer to her. They were curious or maybe they liked the calm around her now. One butterfly fluttered closer and closer and then landed softly on her shoulder. Its wings gently moved up and down.

This moment taught her that when you stop chasing after things and sit quietly, listening and watching, the things you want might just come to you on their own. It was a magical day for the girl, not just because she made a new friend, but also because she learned that patience and peace could bring her closer to the beauty of the world around her.

Just as the girl in the garden learned that stillness and patience could invite beauty and insight, our own journeys often reveal that moments of connection and shifts in perspective can lead to profound changes. My experience on a selling team during the bustling Christmas season serves as an example of this.

Faced with health issues that isolated me from my team and confined me to a solitary role at an airport, I felt detached and undervalued. Removed from my team's camaraderie, I often felt isolated. It seemed unfair, and I felt as if my efforts were worthless compared to my teammates.

However, the universe has a way of sending us exactly what we need at the right moment. For me, it was a chance encounter with someone I admired. This interaction, brief as it might have been, ignited a seismic shift in my mindset. Suddenly, the negativity that clouded my thoughts was swept away and replaced by a wave of newfound confidence. My spirit was uplifted and calm. Gratitude filled the void left by despair, transforming my outlook entirely.

As the season transitioned into the new year, the impact of this shift became unmistakably clear. Not only did my health improve, allowing me to reunite with my team, but my approach to selling was revitalized. My performance soared, even during the challenging post-Christmas period when sales typically dwindled.

This experience reinforced a critical lesson. Our thoughts influence our reality. It's not the external circumstances or others' actions that shape our success and well-being, but our perceptions and reactions. I altered my outcomes by quieting my thoughts.

This journey, much like the metaphorical dance of parenting teens with the map of FROGS, highlights how flexibility, rapport, and simple, positive conversations can significantly alter outcomes. Whether it's nurturing the growth of a teen or facing personal hurdles, the essence of our experiences reinforces the importance of staying open to change and the power of human connection. In both cases, it's these moments of insight and shifts in perspective that paved the way for growth and improvement.

Clarity and Connections

In this journey, embracing the values of truth, beauty, and goodness plays a crucial role. Accessing truth through our inner wisdom brings about heartfelt connections. It guides us and teens to embrace sincerity in our interactions, nurturing a trust that is both profound and lasting. This journey of inner discovery encourages us to listen to our intuitive voice. The value of authentic communication is found in vulnerability. By tapping into this deep well of understanding, we foster an environment where trust flourishes, binding us with bonds that are not only enduring but also enriched by the wisdom that comes from truly knowing and accepting one another.

Beauty goes beyond what we see. It's found in the laughter shared over a family dinner, the quiet moments of understanding when words are unnecessary, and the shared experiences that bring us joy. It reminds us to appreciate the world around us, finding splendor in the everyday and the extraordinary, nurturing a sense of wonder and appreciation.

Goodness is the kindness we show and the support we offer each other. It's in the helping hand we extend without a second thought and the encouragement we give during tough times. This goodness not only strengthens our family bonds but also guides us toward compassion and empathy in our journeys.

Integrating gratitude into our lives unveils a special kind of magic. It's like opening a window in our minds, making space for joy, appreciation for our loved ones, and a brighter outlook on life. Gratitude enhances our happiness and helps us see the unseen benefit. It turns challenges into opportunities for growth. This mindset not only lifts our spirits but also paves the way for our inner wisdom to blossom.

We all seek a clear mind, understanding that pleasant thoughts foster better results. Our feelings arise from our thoughts rather than our teens' behaviors. Acknowledging this truth simplifies our path and improves our interactions with teens. When we approach them calmly, we nurture a relationship built on respect and closeness. This mindset not only makes our journey smoother but also strengthens the bond we share. It lays the foundation for a deeply connected and supportive family dynamic.

"Dylan's Digital Diary" emphasizes the importance of real-world experiences over digital encounters, advocating for a journey of self-discovery and authentic connections. This narrative is a call to embrace the world's beauty, fostering a life filled with authenticity and meaningful connections. Urging us to reflect on the adventures we miss while scrolling invites us to discover the magic in everyday moments.

After allowing time to reflect on this chapter, step into the next chapter, "Love and Community." This story takes us on a journey of discovering who we are, the power of coming together, and how being real with each other can create a strong, happy community. Enjoy this heartwarming story and see how love and togetherness can change everything.

LOVE AND COMMUNITY

THE PULSE OF LOCAL LIFE RESONATES IN A VIBRANT SUBURBAN community center. This center serves as a hub for self-discovery, inviting teens to explore and reveal their often hidden inner qualities. It's a unique world where the journey of finding one's true self is nurtured and celebrated.

With his remarkable ability to connect, Mark helps the town's youth feel more vibrant and engaged. He envisions the center as more than a place for fun; it's a safe haven where teens can feel supported and valued. Through workshops that he organizes, teens have opportunities to share their stories and collaborate on creative projects, fostering a sense of community and belonging.

His commitment to the center is transformative, inspiring teens as they navigate their hopes and uncertainties. Under Mark's guidance, they see a mentor who brings innovative ideas and vitality to the community, making it a more dynamic and supportive environment.

Connecting Through Digital Tales

In the heart of the neighborhood, the community center, once quiet, started buzzing with excitement because of Mark's new idea. People from all around came with cameras and notepads, ready to tell their own stories through videos and photos. They shared about things they love, their challenges, and the happy moments that make life special. This project was about more than telling stories. It helped everyone feel closer to each other.

One story that stood out was about Ariella and her dad, Jonathon. Ariella talked about how trying to look perfect on social media made her feel lonely. Sharing this opened Jonathon's eyes to how different things are now from when he was young. Their honest talk started important conversations at the center about how social media can make us feel and how important it is to be ourselves, both online and in real life.

Mark started workshops to help everyone improve their story-telling. Teachers and storytellers came to teach, turning the community center into a fun place where people of all ages could learn and share.

But mixing digital stories with real-life chats was tricky. Mark wanted to keep the warmth of talking face-to-face while using modern technology. With help from the community's ideas, he worked hard to make sure technology brought people together, not apart. He even raised money to get more computers for the center and started classes so everyone could join in, no matter how much they knew about tech before.

The community center became a lively place where people could share and connect. "It's all about bringing people together," Mark would say, his passion evident in his eyes. No matter what the weather was outside, the center was a warm spot full of chat and laughter.

Mark introduced roundtable chats as a cozy way for everyone at the community center to share their thoughts and stories. It was important to him that each person felt heard and valued. Rosa, known for her wisdom and sense of humor, often took the lead in these discussions. With a warm smile, she'd remind everyone, "Our stories link us together, even if they're a bit messy." Her words set the tone for open, heartfelt sharing, where people felt safe expressing their true selves, warts and all.

During one of these roundtable sessions, Laura, a single mom, opened up about her struggles and victories. "Life's hard, but we're moving forward together. You're not alone," she shared, her voice steady and sincere. Her story, filled with challenges and resilience, struck a chord with many at the center. It wasn't just her words but the courage behind them that inspired others. Laura's openness became a beacon of hope, showing that even in tough times, the community's support could make a difference.

Then, there was Jake, a teenager who usually kept to himself, finding it hard to open up. However, the center, under Mark's guidance, became a place where he discovered his voice through music. "I never thought I could just be myself in front of others," Jake admitted after performing a song he wrote. His music spoke of his fears and dreams, resonating with many who felt the same way but hadn't found the words. Jake's journey from a shy teen to a confident musician inspired his peers to explore and share their own talents and stories.

These roundtable chats, initiated by Mark, became much more than just discussions. They were sessions of shared humanity, where laughter, tears, and everything in between were welcomed. Rosa's leadership, Laura's resilience, and Jake's breakthrough highlighted the center's role as a nurturing ground for growth, self-discovery, and community spirit. Through these gatherings, Mark's vision of a tightly knit, supportive community came to life, proving that when people come together to share their stories, they find strength in their common experiences and hope for the future.

Journey of Authenticity

Mark's genuine care and innovative ideas have turned the center into a warm, buzzing place that feels like a second home to many. Mark's leadership is all about being true to oneself and understanding everyone's unique needs, making the center a peaceful spot full of understanding and friendship, quite different from places where arguments are more common.

Mark really connected with some thoughts on being authentic, shared by thinkers like Kernis and Goldman.[1] These ideas didn't just stay in his head. They became the heart of everything he did at the center and in his own life.

The idea of "Know Yourself" hit home for Mark. He saw how important it is to look beyond our online profiles to find our real selves. This became a big message at the center, with Mark encouraging both kids and adults to dig deep and discover their true values and beliefs. "Finding out who you are beyond the screen is the first step to really growing," Mark would often share, sparking deep thoughts and conversations among visitors.

With "See Clearly," Mark embraced looking at himself honestly, recognizing both his strengths and things on which he could work. He shared this open-minded approach with everyone at the center, building a place where it's okay to be imperfect. "We all have things to work on, and that's okay. It's part of learning and getting better," Mark would say, helping everyone feel okay about sharing their own struggles and successes.

"Walk the Talk" came to life in how Mark made sure the center's actions matched its values. He led by example, showing respect, empathy, and honesty weren't just kind words but actions to live by.

"What we do here shows what we believe in," Mark would remind his team, teaching young people the value of aligning what they do with what they believe in.

Being "Real with Others" was vital to how Mark connected with people. He made the center a place where real, heartfelt talks happen all the time, making everyone feel they could indeed be themselves. "Real friendships happen when we're honest with each other," Mark believed.

Mark put these ideas into action and changed how things worked at the center. Mark set up workshops and fun activities that let people drop the masks they wear online or in society, helping them do activities that show off their real likes and talents. He brought in painting classes where folks could show their feelings without having to use words and story times where everyone could share their real-life stories openly.

Also, Mark made sure the center was a place where it was okay to be open about your worries and hopes. He started groups where both teens and grown-ups could talk about what's on their minds in a friendly and supportive space. These groups, with a vision to do service projects, also helped younger and older participants get to know and support each other.

Mark's way of doing things had an enormous impact, changed lives and brought people closer together. Under Mark's guidance, the center is more than just a place for activities. It's a space for discovering oneself and building strong community bonds.

Inner Wisdom, Community Harmony

Mark made a discovery that changed everything for him and the community he cared for. He learned about the inside-out way of thinking, realizing that the key to real change and understanding starts from within. This idea became clear to him as he tackled the difficulties of running the center, turning it into a place full of hope and connection.

Embracing this inside-out perspective, Mark began to apply it not just to himself but also in his approach to leading the community. He saw that true transformation begins with an individual's internal shift. This shift could influence everything from the way people communicate to how they solve problems together. It was about more than just finding solutions. It was about creating an environment where everyone could discover their own inner strength and wisdom. Mark's realization that changes start from within encouraged everyone at the center to reflect on their own thoughts and feelings, leading to deeper connections and a stronger community fabric.

Mark understood that the wisdom and clarity he needed weren't out there somewhere. They were already inside him, just waiting to be found. This understanding helped him see his job in a new light. Instead of just reacting to problems based on what he thought he knew or what others expected, he learned to stop and listen softly to his inner wisdom. This way of thinking brought him peace and confidence, even when things were tough.

This novel approach made an enormous difference to the center's projects. For example, when Mark started the digital story-telling project, not everyone was sure it was a clever idea. Instead of arguing or trying to convince them with just facts, Mark looked inward. He thought about the real goal of the project. It was to help people understand each other better and bring them closer, using stories shared through technology as a bridge.

Mark's inner wisdom led him to create spaces where people could openly discuss their doubts and hopes. He set up workshops that focused on how to listen softly and connect with each other's stories, not just the technical side of making them. This helped everyone feel part of the project, bringing different generations together around their shared stories.

Mark also showed how important it is to lead with your heart and be true to yourself. He became a leader who deeply cared about his community's growth and happiness. This genuine approach made a significant impact, encouraging others to also listen softly within themselves for their answers and ways to connect.

By following this path, Mark didn't just find personal happiness. He also inspired those around him to explore their own inner worlds. The community center became more than a place for fun activities. It turned into a sanctuary for personal exploration and growth, helping to create a stronger, more understanding community.

Mark's story shows us how digging deep for wisdom inside us can actually change things for the better. Turning the community center into a lively spot full of creativity and togetherness highlights what can happen when we listen to our inner wisdom.

The Joy of Being You

Mark stood in front of the community center. His voice calm yet full of passion. "Think of this place as a sanctuary," he began, his eyes sweeping over the gathered crowd. "A place where we celebrate every little step forward, without casting shadows on our journey by comparing it to others."

A young woman, looking thoughtful, raised her hand. "But Mark, how do we stop the comparisons? They seem automatic."

Mark smiled gently. "It starts within," he said. "By recognizing that it's okay not to be perfect. Every mistake is a lesson, not a failure. We grow, together, from these lessons."

Later, inside the center, Mark continued, "Here, we can be our true selves. There's no room for fear of judgment. It's about being kind to yourself, changing negative thoughts into positive actions."

A man in the back, inspired, shared, "I've always been tough on myself, expecting too much. How do you suggest we start forgiving ourselves?"

Mark nodded, acknowledging the question. "Self-forgiveness is like tending a garden," he explained. "You have to clear away the weeds of self-doubt and plant seeds of kindness and understanding. It's a process, removing the heavy stuff to let new thoughts grow."

He paused, letting his words sink in. "Remember, every new day is a chance to improve. Following this path won't erase all challenges, but it will give us a kinder heart to face them."

As the meeting came to a close, Mark left them with one final thought. "Choosing kindness and forgiveness toward ourselves strengthens our community. It fills us with the joy of being comfortable with who we are. Let's make that our goal."

The room erupted in applause, with the community united by Mark's vision.

———

As Mark talked about the power of forgiving oneself, people let go of trying to be perfect and being too hard on themselves. By doing this, not only did it make things easier for individuals, but it also made the community center a friendlier, more supportive place.

Imagine two friends who started feeling jealous of each other, making things awkward between them. Mark helped people see that they didn't have to stick to those feelings. They could choose to stop comparing themselves and accept who they were. He told them to let go of those thoughts so they wouldn't ruin their happiness. It didn't fix everything, but it made it easier to deal with challenges with a kind heart. Letting go of negative thoughts about oneself also made people more open to change.

Mark's approach at the community center not only fostered self-discovery but also cultivated a deep sense of community. By encouraging everyone to listen to their inner voice and value their own worth independent of external opinions, a genuinely supportive and nurturing environment emerged. This foundation of mutual understanding and care allowed everyone at the center to thrive together.

New Spin on Marriage

Building on this narrative of personal growth and community transformation, let's explore the unique aspects of the Holy Blessing Ceremony. This event redefines traditional concepts of marriage, prompting us to reconsider our views on love, promises, and community involvement. It invites couples to join a global family, emphasizing a commitment to broader societal values. This ceremony is about returning to the essence of love and collaborating towards a harmonious world. Understanding the power of this ceremony can inspire us to see how love can drive positive change, enhancing our lives and the world around us.

When I first encountered the concept of the Holy Blessing, it shifted my perspective on love and commitment. This ceremony is about entering a relationship with the intention of building a future together, guided by the virtues of truth, beauty, and goodness. It's a pledge made in the presence of what I refer to as the Heavenly Parent, signifying a bond that extends beyond personal affection to encompass a shared mission of contributing positively to the world.

The Blessing Ceremony stands out by involving hundreds or even thousands of couples in a collective vow, emphasizing that marriage is about more than individual happiness. It's a step toward building stronger communities and a more peaceful world.

Why do this with so many others? By coming together in marriage, we're connecting families and cultures. It's a way of saying we're all in this together, aiming for a world filled with more love.

Since the first Blessing Ceremony by Rev. and Mrs. Moon in 1960, this idea has reached all the continents in the world, bringing together people from every kind of background. What's amazing is how everyone is welcome, including people of different faiths and races, all coming together because they believe in love, peace, and making life better for everyone.

Participating in the Blessing Ceremony transformed my view of relationships and the essence of making a lifelong commitment. Being part of a larger pursuit to foster a caring and connected world has intensified the joy in our relationship. It has been a journey of love and hope. I'm honored and happy to be on this path.

Think of a regular marriage like your favorite song. It's comfortable and familiar, and everyone knows the words. Now, imagine the Holy Blessing Ceremony as a remix of that song. It's got a fresh beat and new energy, making an old favorite feel exciting again.

In a traditional marriage, two people come together, promise to stick by each other and start their journey. It's like playing a video game where each person has their own controller and screen. They're playing together but on their individual paths.

The Holy Blessing Ceremony is different. It's like playing a game on the same screen, working together every step of the way. This ceremony is all about building a life together with a shared vision. It's more than just being side by side. It's creating something special together.

This ceremony takes what's great about marriage—love, promises, and teamwork—and turns it up a notch. It's about choosing to blend our lives in a way that improves both of us and the world around us. It's a promise not just to live together but to thrive together, making a story about two people being stronger as one.

Connecting with the bigger picture of the universe on our own is like finding a secret level in a game. It's about seeing how we fit into a bigger world and using that knowledge to grow and find our way. It's a journey of self-discovery, understanding who we are and where we're headed.

When a couple does this together, it's like joining forces in a big online game. They're not just using their own skills. They're tapping into a bigger pool of wisdom and love. This connection shows them that their relationship is more than just the two of them. It's part of something vast and connected. The Holy Blessing symbolizes a journey from the shadows into the light for couples. It represents a delightful return to innocence and unity,

If you want to explore the Holy Blessing further, please visit our resources page for additional information. https://www.upliftingedu cation.com/resources

The Holy Blessing Ceremony opens a gateway for couples and communities alike, encouraging a commitment to grander causes and paving the way for the experience of authentic love. Inspired by this kind of spirit, Mark infused similar principles into his work at the community center.

He initiated a series of community service projects, inviting families to engage in activities that benefitted the broader community, such as organizing neighborhood clean-ups and volunteering at local shelters. These endeavors not only fostered a sense of responsibility and compassion among participants but also highlighted the importance of contributing to something greater than oneself.

Love, Teens, and Harmony

Good parenting, a happy marriage, and a community that rocks all need loads of patience, trying to understand where the other person is coming from, and wanting to grow together. Taking time to chill and listen to what our hearts say can give us innovative ideas on how to connect better. This way, we can really get what our teens or spouses are going through so we can provide them with the support they *need*.

Balancing online life with the real world is a big challenge in our fast-paced world. Being real in how we connect with others is super important. Creating a peaceful and supportive environment at home and in our community starts with really listening to each other. How can we ensure teens feel listened to and supported, encouraging honest talks and understanding in our family and beyond?

Thinking about these kinds of questions helps us start working toward building stronger ties in our families and communities. Like how the Blessing Ceremony brings people together to make the world better, using these ideas in our family life can make our bonds deeper and give us a bigger vision.

The Inner Connection Quest leads us on a journey to discover our original selves and to live authentically, reminding us that this path is not one we walk alone. It blossoms from our individual reflections and through actively engaging with our community. Let's rethink how we manage parenting, marriage, and improving our communities, focusing on softly listening to our hearts and committing to trust, respect, and valuing one another. This way, we're not only supporting teens through their challenges but also creating a happier, more united world.

Coming up in the next chapter, we'll meet the Harpers. Get ready to see how their adventures and challenges bring them closer and spread positivity around their neighborhood. It's a heartwarming tale that might inspire you and your family to team up and make a difference, too!

CHAPTER 12
SEEDS OF IMPACT

As the morning sun floods the Harper's living room with light, making the family photos on the walls glow, Maggie is deeply engaged in her painting, each brushstroke reflecting her love for nature.

In a lively contrast, Calvin zips around, dribbling a soccer ball with astonishing skill. His laughter and playful shouts fill the space, imagining himself as the star player scoring the decisive goal in a major game.

Their parents, Kevin and Danielle, watch their children's diverse worlds from the sidelines, exchange a look of amusement and pride.

Kevin asks Maggie, "Hey, what do you think about a community event or how about a charity fundraiser where we combine your art and your brother's soccer skills to help make our environment healthier."

Maggie looks up, her interest piqued, "You mean, use my paintings for a gallery show?" Her usual calmness turns into excitement and a bit of nervousness at the idea.

Calvin stops mid-dribble. "Any chance to play soccer sounds good to me."

Danielle agrees. "It sounds intriguing having different talents come together for a great cause."

As the family gathers, brainstorming and bouncing ideas off each other, the room buzzes with a new energy. Plans for the event start to take shape, driven by a mix of creativity, sportsmanship, and a shared desire to make a difference.

Uniting Worlds

As the Harper family continued planning their special charity event, their home became a lively hub of excitement and planning. But soon, they hit a snag.

Maggie starts feeling anxious. "I want to help, but showing my art to everyone is kinda scary."

Kevin and Danielle got it. Maggie's art is super personal to her, like sharing a diary.

Danielle suggests. "What if we have a small showcase at home first? Just family and a few friends to get you used to the idea."

Maggie is okay with the idea of a safe, familiar crowd. Soon, their living room is rearranged into a cozy art space, displaying Maggie's work like a personal journey in paint.

The night of this small show brings smiles and support. As they admire Maggie's art, their kind words and constructive comments help her fear fade away. She starts to see her art from their perspective, feeling a connection she hadn't anticipated. This mini exhibit ends up boosting her confidence, preparing her for the bigger event.

Calvin, full of ideas for his soccer event, hits his own roadblock with the details. Organizing turns out to be trickier than he thought.

Seeing his struggle, Kevin brings paper and markers and suggests, "Let's map this out."

Kevin shows Calvin the importance of delegating. "Think of it as being the one who sees the whole game and knows where to pass the ball," he says.

This clicks for Calvin. He realizes organizing is not so different from playing soccer.

Challenges and Victories

The Harper household became a hive of activity and nervous energy as the event date drew nearer. The once calm and organized plans seemed to quiver under the weight of impending reality. Maggie became increasingly haunted by the fear of public judgment. Meanwhile, Calvin, usually the epitome of positivity, was clouded by anxiety over the unpredictability of the weather, a factor that could derail his soccer match.

Sensing the growing tension, Kevin and Danielle called for a family meeting one evening, gathering everyone in the living room where the journey had begun. The familiar comfort of the room, with Maggie's paintings adorning the walls and soccer memorabilia scattered around, served as a reminder of the family's unity and strength.

"Maggie, Calvin, we want you both to know that the value of this event isn't solely in its success but in the effort and passion you're putting into it," Kevin began. His voice was steady and reassuring.

Danielle added, "Your worth isn't defined by how others perceive your work or things beyond your control, like the weather. It's about the courage to share a part of yourself and the willingness to step up for a cause you believe in."

Maggie listened intently. Her mother's words resonated within her, touching a chord. She realized that her art, an extension of her inner self, was valuable regardless of public opinion. It was a medium through which she could connect with others, share her perspective, and contribute to a cause close to her heart.

Calvin, leaning forward, took in his father's comforting presence. The realization dawned that his efforts in organizing the match were already a display of leadership and commitment. The unpredictable weather couldn't wash away the fact that he had brought people together for a worthy cause.

The family meeting turned into a discussion about personal worth and the intrinsic value of their contributions. Kevin and Danielle shared stories of their challenges and how they had learned to find value in their endeavors, irrespective of the outcomes.

As the meeting drew to a close, Maggie and Calvin felt a renewed sense of purpose. They were reminded that their value didn't hinge on the perfect execution of the event or the acclaim it received but lay in their willingness to put themselves out there for something they believed in.

The following days saw Maggie and Calvin moving forward with a newfound sense of confidence. They were no longer preparing for a charity event but embarking on a journey of self-discovery and affirmation of their inner value.

The night before their big day, the family gathered not to plan but to cherish their time together, reinforcing the close bonds that had supported them all along. As they retired to bed that evening, they felt a sense of calm. With the showcase yet to begin, they slept not merely as individuals ready to display their talents, but as a family, united in purpose.

The Harper Event

The morning of the Harper family's big charity event was sunny and full of promise, stirring up excitement and some last-minute nerves at their house. As the sun came up, everyone was already up and about, getting ready for the day ahead.

Maggie carefully packed her art, feeling a mix of nerves and excitement about showing her work to the community. The idea of everyone seeing her paintings made her anxious, but remembering how well her small show went at home gave her courage.

As Calvin stood on the edge of the soccer field, his excitement quickly turned to frustration as voices around him rose in a heated debate. "Hey, I thought I was on the red team!" one player shouted, pointing accusingly at another.

"No way, we decided this last week," another retorted, his face flushed with anger.

Calvin, trying to mediate, felt overwhelmed. "Guys, please, let's just play fair. We can figure this out," he attempted, but his words seemed to drown in the sea of disagreement.

Seeing his son's distress from the sidelines, Kevin approached with a calm demeanor. "Calvin, you're doing great, but it looks like things are getting a bit heated. Need a hand?"

Calvin, visibly relieved, nodded. "Yeah, Dad, I could really use some help."

Together, they faced the disgruntled players. Kevin, with a reassuring presence, addressed the group. "Let's take a moment, everyone. It's important we all enjoy the game and remember why we're here today. Disagreements can happen, but it's how we handle them that counts."

Calvin took a deep breath and addressed the players with newfound confidence. "Okay, let's talk this through. We're all here to have fun and support a worthy cause, right?"

The tension began to ease as the players started to listen to each other, guided by Calvin and Kevin's calm approach. The argument that had seemed so big moments before was resolved through patience and understanding, turning the potential discord into a lesson in diplomacy and teamwork.

As the event kicked off, Maggie's art turned one part of the community center into a mini art gallery. People seemed really into it and talking to them about her paintings made Maggie feel proud and a bit more confident, even after a tough critique from a local artist shook her a little at first.

Outside, Calvin's soccer game was a hit, bringing everyone together and making the day feel special. Then, suddenly, it started raining hard, threatening to stop the game. But Calvin didn't let that dampen their spirits. He quickly moved everyone indoors so the game could keep going, turning a potential letdown into a highlight of the day.

Finding Calm, Gaining Clarity

As the Harper family settled into their living room, Kevin initiated a conversation that drew everyone closer. "Today was more than just about the event, wasn't it?" he mused, looking at Maggie and Calvin with a mixture of curiosity and pride.

Maggie nodded, her eyes reflecting a mixture of fatigue and satisfaction. "Definitely. I mean, at first, all I could think about was how my art would be received. But then, when I saw people genuinely connecting with it, discussing it... it was like I could calm down and think about them. I realized it's not just about the art itself, but the conversations it starts."

Calvin chimed in; his usually energetic demeanor softened by the day's reflections. "Yeah, and on the field, it wasn't just the game. It's weird, but I saw how bringing people together for a worthy cause is a win in itself. It was like when I stopped worrying about scoring or winning, I actually played better."

Danielle smiled, adding, "It sounds like both of you discovered that sometimes, stepping back and finding a moment of peace can bring clarity and wisdom. It's not just about the doing, but also being confident about who we are and appreciating the moment."

Kevin nodded. "Exactly, and it's a lesson for all of us. The chaos before today, and then the calmness now, is all part of the journey. By embracing the calm, we open ourselves up to learning and growing, not just as individuals but together, as a family."

The room was filled with a sense of unity and camaraderie. Through their shared experiences, the Harpers had learned that amidst the hustle of life, finding moments of calm could lead to insights and strengthen the bonds between them. This conversation marked not just the end of a successful day but the beginning of a deeper family connection.

From Sapling to Oak

When our kids were growing up, our home became a lot like the Harper family's. Daily life turned into this always-changing classroom filled with chances to learn and grow. Our garden, which was colorful and alive, was more than just a nice spot to hang out. It became a real-life lab for learning about horticulture.

Just across our driveway, my brother was the cool uncle, teaching all the cousins the ABCs of agriculture and farm life, from nurturing plants to looking after animals. It was like having our own live-action homesteading tutorial, and no YouTube needed!

But the learning continued beyond the garden gate. Take our porch project, for example. It wasn't just a makeover. It was a masterclass in patience, effort, and the thrill of progress. Strokes of paint and swipes of the sandpaper were lessons in sticking with it. They showed us how small steps can lead to impressive changes. Projects, no matter how small, teach patience, precision, and the satisfaction of transforming something with your own hands.

Our way of learning, which valued helping others, strengthened our awareness and resilience in the process. It became a way to experience real-world lessons and grasp what others are going through. Every project, whether it was joining in local beach clean-ups or renovating school properties in Mexico, helped us see how we fit into the bigger picture.

Planting a tree became our emblem of responsibility and growth. Those trees, standing tall through storms and sunshine, became symbols of how our actions ripple out, providing shade and resting places for wildlife.

When teens decide to plant trees, for example, it's not just about them getting their hands dirty. Service learning is an entry ticket for the Inner Connection Quest. It's about digging deep into what lights them up and discovering how they can spark change in the world.

By choosing to plant trees or doing another type of practical service, teens are doing more than just gardening or helping out. They're planting their dreams, values, and commitments into the earth. They're learning life's critical lessons. Then, they can see the ripple effect of their actions. This hands-on journey is their crash course in making small moves for big impacts.

For families, it's good to remember that doing things together, like planting a tree or getting involved in a project for the community, shows the strength and possibility in all of us. These shared moments are more than just activities. They are important experiences that bring us closer, teaching us about toughness, togetherness, and the joy of working toward a common goal.

When we plant a tree together, it's not just about the action of replanting. It's about setting down a living symbol of growth, hope, and the future. This simple act is full of deeper meanings about life. Trees stand firm through storms, growing through tough times, reaching up toward the light, just like we do. They show us how to face hard moments, overcome them, and aim for our dreams. Every time we take care of that tree, seeing it grow, it reminds us of our growth, our strength, and how sticking together, grounded in love and support, makes us stronger.

Taking part in community projects as a family does something similar. It ties our family's story into the bigger story of our community. These projects are like mirrors that show the good change happening inside each of us as we help change the world around us. It's about helping ourselves as we help others, learning to understand and care for others, and finding happiness in giving. We see that our family, working as one, can do a lot of good, shining as a light of change and hope.

These experiences are like anchors keeping us stable through life's hills and valleys. They remind us that, even though life can be tough, we won't break. Instead, we'll become stronger, more able to deal with challenges, and more closely tied to what we truly value day by day. Just like the roots of a tree grow deeper to stand up to wind and rain, our family's roots of love, support, and shared values get stronger, creating a bond that can get through anything life throws at us.

This tree-planting example is more than a lesson in science. It's a quest for meaning, revealing teens' inner worth and the superhero power they have to have influence. And the best part? They get to watch their tree and their impact grow over time. So, cheers to the simple act of planting a tree or another service project! It's proof that little steps can lead to grand adventures in personal growth.

Wisdom in the Slow Lane

The Harper family's story highlights how important it is to be open to change and to grow with each other. This mindset is critical not just for making family ties stronger but also for making everyone's lives better and having a pleasant effect on the people around us. Starting to think in new ways opens up deeper understanding. As we listen softly for inner wisdom, we start seeing situations more clearly. Being present in the moment helps us figure out the best things to say and the most productive responses to connect with others.

In our Inner Connection Quest toward wisdom, the process of calming down becomes a bridge to discovery. It's like navigating a river that flows within us, steering through the currents of immediate reactions to find the tranquil waters of deeper insight. This serene state enables us to tap into a well of knowledge that often lies untapped, overshadowed by the hustle of our daily lives.

In these moments of quietude, we can hear the whispers of our own experiences and values, guiding us toward choices that reflect who we are at our core. This internal guidance system is invaluable, especially when navigating the complex dynamics of family life and the challenges of connecting with teens. In this stillness, we can often find the answers for which we've been searching.

When teens challenge us with harsh words, taking a moment to pause before reacting allows our minds to clear, making room for insight to guide our responses. This approach involves being flexible in our responses, seeking understanding, aiming for positive outcomes, and keeping our conversations authentic.

Similar to how we encourage a child learning to walk, we can understand that stumbling is part of growth. In connecting with teens, facing these challenges without fear and focusing on understanding them can ease our own concerns, enabling us to adapt and forge stronger bonds. By offering our patience and support, we nurture a relationship that is both strong and filled with mutual respect.

Life's challenges often prompt a "why me?" attitude, overlooking the resilience and intelligence life can stimulate. Shifting our perspective to trust in a greater good changes our outlook, opening us to receive love and support that inspires us with strength and wisdom. The realization that we're only a thought away from a better mindset or solving a problem is profound. However, in the midst of adversity, it's challenging to recognize the "gifts" these situations bring. Typically, it's only in retrospect that we appreciate the growth and learning they've facilitated.

It's valuable to understand how our thoughts work. A calm mind lets us be more creative, hopeful, and strong, while a busy mind can drag us down. We hear our inner wisdom more clearly when our minds aren't racing and we can listen softly.

Think about driving. At a reasonable speed, driving is enjoyable, but going too fast makes it hard to enjoy the ride. When everything feels stressful, slowing down lets us appreciate the moment and enjoy the scenery.

If we keep going at an accelerated pace, like 50 mph, it's manageable, but we'll need a break after a while. Push our minds too hard for too long, and we'll definitely need some time off. Otherwise, we'll burn out.

Driving at 100 mph or letting our thoughts race at this speed gets overwhelming. We'll require a break before long and we'll see the effects of tension physically and mentally.

At 200 mph, we'll see warning lights on the car's dashboard, which is if we don't get stopped by the police first. A mind that is busy can lead to constant worry, making bad choices, and feeling overwhelmed. Physical and mental symptoms from excessive strain are signs that we need to slow down our thoughts.

Ignoring these stress signs can make us feel even worse, stuck in a loop of tension and thinking that can make every day a struggle. If we slow our thoughts down to a calm pace, life gets more simple and pleasant, especially if we're used to the chaos of super-fast thinking.

So, do we choose stress and its tough consequences, or do we decide to take it more lightly for a healthier, happier life? Paying attention to how fast our thoughts are racing lets us choose how we want to feel. Once we pick a pace that feels good, our minds will adjust, leading to a more balanced life. For parents, showing this calm way of living not only helps us but also shows teens how to have a more sensible and pleasant life.

In wrapping up this journey of growth, resilience, and deep-rooted connection, let's remember the power of meaningful conversations within our families, much like the Harper family displayed. Delving into thoughtful questions can transform simple chats into bridges of understanding where everyone feels valued and important.

Two pivotal questions to spark engaging dialogues might be: What are some ways we can make sure everyone in our family feels listened to and appreciated for their unique talents? Or, how do you think helping others in the community makes us grow or change as individuals and as a family?

Let's keep asking questions, cheering for each other's unique abilities, and embracing community service as a pathway to transformation. By doing so, we nurture a legacy of strength, empathy, and connectedness, inspiring not just our own family but also igniting a chain reaction of positive impact everywhere.

As we continue to the fourth part of this book, called "Innerconnectedness," we take a special trip. But this trip isn't to far-off places. Instead, we explore the wide world inside our hearts and minds. And that's not all. We also learn how to spread this joy around, creating ripples of heartfelt connections in our relationships and communities.

PART FOUR

INNERCONNECTEDNESS

The Inner Connection Quest focuses on important qualities like truth, beauty, and goodness. By paying close attention to our feelings, thoughts, and choices, we can improve our inner health. This helps us connect better with the world around us and the people in it. It's all about making our relationships richer and continuing to grow these connections throughout our lives.

THREADS OF CONNECTION

Ah, the good old days when the toughest choice was chocolate or vanilla, and the scariest thing was the monster lurking under the bed. Fast forward to when teens are navigating through a jungle of self-esteem issues, friendship dramas, and the big quest of figuring out who they are. Yet, at the heart of it all, every teen wants to feel like they matter, that they're a VIP in the story of life.

A Mosaic of Moments

Picture a brisk afternoon in Paris, the Louvre calling out to art buffs from around the globe. There, among the masterpieces by legends like Da Vinci, we find a tapestry, an ancient woven story. To a casual observer, it's a grand depiction, showing a slice of history or a myth. But, as any art enthusiast says, the real magic is in the tiny details.

Step right up, and this tapestry unfolds a story of thousands of threads, each one twirled and twisted under the careful guidance of an expert craftsperson. Colors blend together, designs pop to life, and shapes emerge, all because of these little threads.

Alone, a single thread might look weak or dull. From a short distance, its unique shade might not stand out. Likewise, in our lives, some moments or decisions might seem small or unimportant on their own. We might be quick to write them off as nothing special.

But the true beauty of the tapestry, its story, comes not from individual threads but from how they intertwine. Some threads stretch everywhere, others are short and sweet, yet each one is crucial, supporting its neighbors and giving the tapestry its strength and beauty. This is a reflection of our communities, where everyone, no matter how different, comes together in beautiful harmony.

Imagine our lives as a vibrant tapestry telling the story of who we are. Now the picture removes just one thread. At first, it might not seem important, but soon we realize that the tapestry's story is now incomplete. Each person, much like every thread, adds a unique touch to the human story. Missing even one person can disrupt the entire balance.

Our lives are complex stories crafted from relationships and experiences. It's easy to focus on the big picture and overlook the minor details. However, it's often these small moments that truly capture the essence of our lives. By valuing each thread, each moment, we can guide teens through their transformative years with love, laughter, and wisdom.

Innerconnectedness takes us on an intriguing journey to uncover the interconnected web of our thoughts, emotions, and experiences. It can be compared to revealing a secret map that illustrates how these inner elements shape our identity and influence how we interact with the world. Teens can start to see how challenges they face, victories they celebrate, and moments they live add pieces to the puzzle of their lives, crafting the magnificent tapestry that represents their unique identity.

This journey of self-discovery encourages us to tune in to our inner voice, embracing the idea that a teen's individuality is their superpower. Their distinctive stories can have the influence of leaving a lasting mark on the world.

Weaving Confidence Together

The delicate threads of connection weave a story of belonging and significance during adolescence, a time when these threads may loosen, plunging teens into a storm of doubt and uncertainty.

"Why does it feel like I just don't fit in anywhere?" a teen might ask, looking up from the glow of social media that amplifies feelings of isolation.

"It's like a social puzzle," a parent might reply, trying to mend the frayed threads of their child's confidence. "Feeling out of place is part of growing up. What truly matters is discovering who you are because your unique self is your true strength. Remember, it's your differences that make you special."

In academics, the pressure can be intense. "I got a C in math. It feels like I'm not good at anything," a teen could confide, feeling their self-worth slip.

"A grade is just a number. It doesn't define you," the parent might encourage, shifting the focus from grades to nurturing inner qualities, "Your personal strengths are what make you shine ."

Identity is the unique blend of qualities, beliefs, and experiences that defines who we are. For teens, developing a clear sense of identity is crucial. It helps them become more independent and make their own decisions.

The digital world adds its own challenges. "Everyone's life looks perfect online, except mine," a teen might sigh, scrolling through endless feeds.

"Remember, online is just a highlight reel, not the full story," a parent might remind them. "Let's find joy in the real world."

Family dynamics can strain connections. "You never listen to me!" a teen might exclaim, feeling overlooked in favor of a sibling.

"Let's talk about it. Your voice matters in our family," a parent could respond, aiming to strengthen the family unit.

Bullying, a shadowy presence, can leave deep scars. "They won't stop posting mean comments about me," a teen might whisper, feeling vulnerable.

"We're here for you. Let's tackle this together. You're not alone," the parent would affirm, offering protection and support.

Softly listening reveals the depth of our connections. "I want to make a difference but don't know how," a teen might share, seeking purpose.

"Being yourself makes a difference. Let's explore what you love and start there," the parent suggests, igniting hope and direction.

Open, judgment-free conversations help teens navigate their complex landscape. "I don't know what I'm good at," a teen might admit.

"We'll discover that together. Every interest is a piece of who you are," the parent encourages, bolstering the teen's sense of identity.

When challenges become overwhelming, professional guidance can offer clarity. "Maybe talking to someone could help me sort things out," a teen might consider.

"That's a brave step forward. Finding someone to talk to can help us find our way," the parent supports, validating the teen's feelings.

Celebrating victories, big or small, enriches a teen's life. "I finished my project on time!" a teen might beam with pride.

"That's wonderful! Let's do something special," the family can celebrate, highlighting the teen's strengths.

Through dialogue, empathy, and guidance, supplemented with professional support when needed, parents can strengthen the fabric of confidence and identity in their teen's life. This ensures that, despite the hurdles, teens emerge stronger, more assured, and confident in their unique place in the world.

Feeling Like I Matter

When I was a teen, while volunteering with my faith group, a kind couple welcomed me, allowing me to feel like part of their family. Then came a significant event. It was an evening filled with tradition and deep conversations held in a beautifully decorated ballroom. Having come from a more laid-back setting, the formality and fancy outfits initially made me feel out of place despite the event's importance.

Afterward, feeling disconnected and small, I found solace in my room at the couple's house. But life had other plans. I was asked to serve water at a small gathering in the dining room, a much cozier scene than the evening's grandeur. The warm chats and laughter among the couple and a few leaders felt like family, a sharp contrast to the night's earlier formality.

As I served water, my mentor's genuine interest in my life made me feel seen and valued. He didn't just lecture; he connected with me like a father would, showing me that I mattered just for being me.

This moment taught me that the heart of our faith isn't in the big events or the strict rules, but in our real, personal connections. It showed me "Innerconnectedness," reminding me that our individual faith stories are woven together with our community's spirit. This realization transformed my perspective on my role within the group, reassuring me that my true value isn't about fitting in.

This experience was a turning point, showing me that every thread, no matter how simple, adds to the community fabric. I started interacting with more confidence and felt a deeper sense of belonging, learning that genuine connections matter more than fitting into grand social scenes.

Together on Two Paths

Teens go through two hero type journeys. The first one is all about dealing with the big and small challenges of growing up. The second journey goes deeper, exploring personal thoughts, feelings, and growth. When we speak about these two hero type journeys of teens, we're referring to two distinct but interconnected paths.

The first, the external journey, deals with the tangible challenges of growing up. It's about things like succeeding in school, forming friendships, and navigating social pressures. There's also overcoming visible obstacles and achieving specific goals that are often recognized and celebrated by others.

The second path, the internal journey, delves deeper into a teen's personal world. It's exploring their thoughts, feelings, and emotional growth. This journey is about self-discovery, understanding and managing emotions, developing a sense of self, and aligning personal values with actions. It focuses on building inner strength and resilience.

Together, these journeys play critical roles in shaping teens into capable and confident individuals equipped to face both the external world and their internal landscapes.

Take the moment when teens have to give a presentation in class. The night before, they share how nervous they are, worrying about messing up in front of everyone. We can offer words of encouragement, suggesting they think of it like an adventure story. We remind them that it's normal to feel scared before facing a big challenge. It's about finding the bravery to go through with it, not avoiding it. And we let them know we're there to support them. This shows how facing tough situations, like speaking in public, helps build strength and bravery.

Then, on a different level, teens talk about feeling unsure about who they are and what the future holds. We can take this chance to comfort them, explaining they're on a journey to discover the deep parts of themselves. We stress that it's fine not to have all the answers immediately. Being curious and asking questions is what's important. Their path will become more evident, one step at a time. This conversation highlights the inward journey's role, focusing on learning about oneself and growing on a personal level. We're here to support teens in navigating their inner world.

These two journeys are intricately connected. The bravery teens show in class feeds into how they see themselves, just like how exploring their inner thoughts affects how they interact with the world. By walking through these journeys with teens, we help them see that the challenges they face and questions they ponder are part of their growth. We encourage them to take both journeys, seeing each step as important in finding out who they are.

Supporting teens means being there, celebrating their successes, and helping them through tough times. We show them that they are the main characters in their own story, both when dealing with the outside world and when discovering their inner self. As they navigate the intricacies of maturation and self-discovery, teens can realize that true growth is about becoming the best version of themselves.

The difference between personal development and spiritual growth enriches this journey further. Personal development is about setting goals and working toward becoming the person we aim to be. It's like the journey outside, where facing and overcoming challenges makes us stronger.

On the other hand, spiritual growth is more about looking inward and letting go of what we've piled on ourselves to find our true essence. It's about reconnecting with who we are and finding happiness in our original nature.

The beauty of these paths lies in how they bring us closer to a deeper connection within ourselves. This inner connection is about understanding and feeling in tune with our true selves beyond just our day-to-day thoughts and actions.

Personal development focuses on our goals and achievements. It's like plotting a course on a map and moving forward, learning new skills, facing challenges, and growing stronger from them. This journey is outward, where we push ourselves to achieve and become who we want to be. It helps us build confidence and resilience, making us feel proud of what we can accomplish.

Spiritual development, on the other hand, invites us to look inward. It's not about adding more achievements or skills but about peeling back layers to reveal who we truly are underneath. This process often involves letting go of beliefs or ideas we've held onto that don't serve us. It's a journey back to our core, to our original nature, where we find peace and contentment in just being ourselves.

When we engage in both personal and spiritual development, we're not just working toward external goals or diving deep into our inner selves. We're doing both to create a richer, more fulfilling experience in life. This dual approach fosters a powerful inner connection, where we're aligned with our actions and our original selves. By balancing these paths, we learn to appreciate our achievements and our journey toward them while also embracing our inherent worth and the peace that comes from simply being.

This inner connectedness influences not just how we see ourselves but also how we interact with the world around us. It encourages a sense of empathy and understanding toward others, as we recognize that everyone is on their own journey. It fosters a deeper appreciation for the interconnectedness of all things, helping us to see the beauty in the world and our place within it.

The beauty of engaging in both personal and spiritual development lies in how they complement each other to deepen our connection with ourselves. This inner connection is the foundation for a life lived with purpose, peace, and a profound sense of belonging to the larger tapestry of existence.

Patterns of Connection

Have you ever thought about what shapes our conversations and self-talk? It's not just the words we exchange but also how we interpret and feel about things. Notice how quickly a heated argument can calm down when someone else, maybe even a child, steps into the room? It shifts right before our eyes from tense to peaceful. This change makes us question how we can quickly switch our emotional gears and release those intense feelings in an instant.

Our emotions come from our thoughts. When we start feeling anxious or angry, it reminds us that these feelings come from inside, not from what's happening around us. If outside people or events were completely controlling our emotions, wouldn't we all react the same way to the same things? Clearly not, since everyone responds differently.

For instance, two friends are stuck in traffic. One might feel frustration, seeing the delay as a bother. The other friend may see it as an opportunity to listen to a favorite podcast and unwind. This difference in perception and reaction shows that our emotions come from inside us, not from what's happening around us.

By consciously choosing to remain calm and present in the moment, we select a new pattern for our emotional tapestry. It promises more tranquility and less turmoil. This choice doesn't just alter our immediate emotional landscape. It reshapes our overall experience and leads us toward a more serene and peaceful state of being.

Sometimes, teens can get on our nerves. Is it really about what they're doing, or is it the colors and textures we think we see? We can sometimes judge them based on what we expect. What if we opened up, put our ego aside, and appreciated the different patterns they're making? It's not about ignoring what they do but understanding that everyone brings their own experiences, making the tapestry of life richer and more colorful.

Memories are moments from our past. The future is a blank space waiting for our next steps. When we're caught up in unhelpful thoughts, focusing on the present helps us. Teens can tell if we're fully engaged with them or just going through the motions.

For instance, when talking to a teen about their hopes for the future, if we're distracted by our worries about their choices, we might not be able to listen softly to what they're dreaming about. By zeroing into their hearts, we can understand their viewpoint and support them in turning their hopes into plans. As they share their ambitions and worries, they're not just talking. They're actively shaping their future. This shared moment, where we connect and share openly, enhances our relationship. It makes our experiences together more meaningful and impactful.

When teens feel ready to share their thoughts and feelings with their parents, their understanding and self-awareness grow. As they share more, it adds vibrancy and connection to our family life.

We all want to feel valued and part of something bigger, contributing in a way that enhances overall beauty. Exploring our feelings and connections in conversations reveals it's more than talk. It's about recognizing and celebrating our impact on each other's lives.

Conversations are about valuing and celebrating each unique person in life's beautiful, ever-growing tapestry. The support I received after the big event in the ballroom allowed me to shift my feeling of inadequacy to a sense of belonging. In the same way, our interactions can enrich the lives around us.

Being a teen is like navigating a maze of emotions, friendships, and discoveries. Recognizing our deep connections helps us see how our feelings and the world intertwine. The journey of Inner Connection is about forging real bonds and understanding each other. Through open conversations, listening, and support, we can equip teens with the tools to weave their special thread into the mix.

Threads of Reflection

To help teens see their value in the interconnected tapestry of life, consider guiding them to document their daily experiences, thoughts, and feelings through journaling or creating a personal blog. This tangible activity offers them a mirror to reflect on their individual journey, highlighting their growth, challenges overcome, and times of joy. We can encourage them to write about or share stories when they felt connected to others, moments of kindness (both given and received), and instances where they made a difference, no matter how small.

As we close this chapter, let's look at how the FROGS map, with its focus on Flexibility, Rapport, Outcome, Grounding, and Simple Conversations, helps us create an environment where teens feel important. Being flexible means changing our plans when things come up, showing we can roll with the punches. Building rapport is like walking together, proving we're in it as a team. Focusing on outcomes gets us to think about the big picture, like imagining the view from a mountain we're climbing. Grounding in our parenting gives teens wisdom from our own experiences, like sharing tips from roads we've already taken. Simple Conversations are those talks that turn the journey into something special.

Each part of the FROGS strategy is key to helping us support teens through their difficulties. Being flexible teaches them to be open to life's twists. Building rapport helps them feel supported and connected. Focusing on outcomes gives them a vision to dream about. Grounding gives them a base of values and a sense of who they are. Simple Conversations create meaningful moments and memories.

Using this approach, we can build a safety net that lets teens know they have a special place in the world. This method doesn't just help teens feel seen and heard. It also makes the journey richer for parents alongside their kids, painting a life full of love, lessons, and close connections.

The Inner Connection Quest is about understanding how our thoughts, feelings, and actions are connected with everything around us. By making sure our conversations with teens show that we understand the importance of their inner world, we're helping them to quietly listen and feel good about themselves.

Gaining insight into how to notice and treasure the small but meaningful moments helps us find joy in the quiet times that often go unnoticed but mean so much to our happiness and well-being. Journaling or blogging is like a mirror for the mind, giving teens (and us!) a chance to reflect on our thoughts and feelings and see how much they can give us joy. This habit offers a space to think about our path and find peace and connection within ourselves.

As we wrap up this chapter through the Threads of Connection, it's clear that adolescence is not just about navigating the challenges of growing up. It's about crafting an identity that resonates deeply with one's true self. From the anxiety of fitting into the pressure of academic achievement and the illusions of social media, each experience threads into the complex tapestry of a teen's life, contributing to their unique pattern of self.

Just like the intricate details that transform a simple piece of fabric into a masterpiece, moments, decisions, and interactions in a teen's life add a rich texture to their evolving story. These experiences, whether they seem monumental or minute, are the fibers that weave together to form the backdrop against which their identity unfolds.

In this digital age, where comparison can cloud our sense of worth, it's more important than ever to remind teens and ourselves of the unique value each of us brings to the world. By fostering open, judgment-free conversations, we not only patch the worn threads of confidence but also reinforce the vibrant hues of individuality that make each teen stand out.

The journey toward recognizing and appreciating one's identity is filled with twists and turns. Yet, it is within this journey that teens learn the power of their own voice, the strength of their convictions, and the beauty of their unique perspective.

As we embrace the challenge of building deeper connections with teens, what lies ahead? The next chapter is called "Harmony in the Hustle." Get ready to discover how finding joy in the simple things can create lasting connections and turn the everyday hustle into harmony.

CHAPTER 14

HARMONY IN THE HUSTLE

An old musician plays his harp in a hustling city center, creating a calm spot amid the city buzz. His music, for those who stop to listen, brings a sense of peace, showing us how we're all connected in our busy lives.

Our lives are like that busy square, filled with non-stop action and loads of information. Yet, at this fast pace, we all look for deeper connections, a calm like the harpist's song amidst the noise.

This search for a happier life might actually be found in the trivial things. Think about the detailed music from the harp. Just like that, the real beauty of life might be in the simple moments that happen every day. These brief times bring depth, color, and joy to our lives.

Let's take a moment to enjoy the simple joys around us. Laughing with friends, seeing a child's wonder, or getting a kind nod from someone can create a beautiful tune. This tune is the key to genuine connection, offering a life filled with meaningful moments that lift us up together.

. . .

Discovering Joy in the Little Things

In a lively forest, a young tree starts its life journey. Just like teens, this tree is surrounded by a world buzzing with life and change. At first, the tree reaches out in every direction, trying to find its place in the sunlight, much like how teens explore various interests, looking for what truly catches their heart.

A significant moment of change arrives when the tree finds a spot bathed in the perfect amount of sunlight. It begins to grow with purpose and focus. Similarly, when teens stumble upon a passion that genuinely interests them, they start to deepen their roots. This process goes beyond just spending time on an activity. It's about diving deep into their heart and mind, connecting with their passion on a meaningful level.

As the tree's roots grow deeper, seeking nutrients, teens, too, start connecting their thoughts, gaining clarity in areas that once seemed unclear. Their path becomes a journey of meaningful exploration, leading them to what they love and pouring their energy into it.

Over time, the sapling transforms into a magnificent tree. Its branches stretch toward the sky. Likewise, teens can delve into their interests and grow in strength and confidence. Their passions shine through, highlighting their unique place in the world.

This tale sheds light on every teen's incredible potential to find joy in the trivial things. They can move beyond fleeting distractions and engage with their interests. Like the tree finding its ideal spot in the sun, teens who discover and dive into their passions connect to themselves and the world around them.

Exploring teenage development, we recognize that individuals have distinct talents and a spirit of curiosity. The teen years are a pivotal time for self-discovery. It's a phase filled with questions about who they are and how they fit into the world. Supporting them through this exploration acknowledges their search for identity, helps them excel in their passions, and encourages creative thinking.

In addition, the path to discovering and nurturing passions is about more than personal growth. It also enables teens to make meaningful contributions to their communities. By encouraging them to find joy in the trivial things and pursue their interests, we're promoting a generation that values deep personal connections and creativity.

When teens lack interest, it's like trying to light a campfire with damp wood. It may be challenging, but not without hope. With patience and understanding, and by encouraging them to notice the joy in the small moments, we can help illuminate their passions. Giving them space to explore and affirm their journey at their own pace is crucial in helping them feel secure and motivated to discover what they love.

Beyond the Solo Journey

The auditorium was alive with energy, filled with the buzz of conversations, the sound of program pamphlets flipping, and the odd nervous cough here and there. Everyone's gaze was fixed on Alex, the high school's top student, who stood confidently at the podium. Yet, behind this moment, Alex's confident demeanor was a complex web of relationships. Every connection on this web had played a part in bringing him to this point.

We often think of our big wins as solo victories. Stories of the lone genius or the self-made success are popular. But looking closer, we see the people around us really shape our paths. Think about the tough mentor who knows just when to push, the friend who's always there, the community that teaches us what's important, or the family that gives us a solid start.

The importance of having people to support us is enormous. Relationships do more than catch us when we fall or light the way; they push us forward, helping us grow and find new directions.

These connections show us that even though we might feel like just one thread, it's the whole network of threads together that makes our lives full and guides us.

Abraham Maslow, a pioneer in understanding human motivation, initially presented a hierarchy of needs, conceptualizing it as a ladder leading towards self-actualization, or reaching our fullest potential.[1] However, Maslow's exploration didn't stop there. He later introduced the concept of self-transcendence, placing it above self-actualization. This advanced stage suggests that ultimate satisfaction is found in going beyond self-centered concerns by engaging with something larger than oneself. It could be contributing to a more significant cause or the benefit of the community.

The teen years are vital for finding a deeper purpose. It's not about fleeting likes or trends for teens. They're on a mission to dig deep, going through all sorts of experiences and challenges to listen softly for what really matters to them. This journey is about more than just discovering meaning. It's about fitting that meaning into their lives and figuring out how their unique experiences are part of everyone's story. This leads them to a rich, connected, and full life.

No matter how small, every step of personal growth links up with others, creating a strong web of experiences. This network shows us that real success is about more than the big moments at the end but all the crucial steps that got us there.

When we think about success, it's a journey full of ups, downs, and determination that shows what we're made of. Significant achievements are just one part of a larger story of growing and becoming who we are.

Embracing Wisdom in Parenting

Parenting teens can seem like trying to spot the hidden image in a Magic Eye™ picture: you only see the deeper picture when you look at it exactly right. This path taps into wisdom that's often lost in our rush to plan every detail. Just like a hidden image that suddenly appears, understanding teens happens in surprising moments, but only if we stop overthinking everything.

To really get to know teens, we have to be genuinely interested in their lives. It's about looking beyond the surface to understand their hopes, fears, and what they dislike. For example, Anita, 15, was afraid of speaking in front of people. Her challenge was about more than getting over this fear. It was about finding confidence. Her parents didn't just offer advice. They really listened to and supported her, which led to Anita's successful speech at school. This was more than just a public speaking win. It was a massive step in Anita's growth.

Teens often feel pulled between wanting to achieve and fearing failure. It's important to understand whether they're chasing concrete achievements or looking for emotional fulfillment. Ryan, 14, wanted to win a tennis tournament not just for the trophy but for the sense of self-esteem and approval it could bring. His parents supported him emotionally, helping him see that self-worth isn't based on victories or what others think. This support was key in helping Ryan build a self-image grounded in his own values, an important skill for facing teenage life.

There are two main ways to set goals: the linear way, which is all about having a clear plan, and the explorer way, which values discovery and flexibility. Alex, 16, is an example of the linear approach, with his detailed plan to become an engineer. My own perspective changed when I started working at a school known for its creative approach to education. This experience showed me the value of the explorer approach, which encourages curiosity and learning through exploration, a stark contrast to my background in structured planning.

At this school, learning wasn't tied to a strict curriculum.

Students were encouraged to pursue their interests, leading to lively and engaged classes. Initially, I found it challenging to adapt my structured goals to this open environment. A conversation with a colleague who had embraced the school's philosophy, helped me see the benefits of a more flexible approach.

An event at the school really opened my eyes to the effectiveness of this philosophy. During a public speaking activity, students supported and encouraged each other in a pressure-free atmosphere. This showed me that growth and learning happen best when there's mutual support and the freedom to explore.

My time at the school taught me that the explorer approach isn't just a way to learn; it's a way to live. It's about enjoying the journey, being open to innovative ideas, and finding joy in every step.

The Power of Pause

Setting goals is like playing a board game like Chutes and Ladders or Monopoly. In both life and games, unexpected surprises, challenges, and opportunities shape the journey. For example, landing on a "Go to Jail" square in Monopoly or sliding down a slide in Chutes and Ladders mirrors setbacks in life, where progress seems halted or reversed. Yet, the game isn't over.

Other times, you might land on a "Chance" card that propels you forward or climb up a ladder, speeding past obstacles. These moments are like life's unexpected opportunities and breakthroughs that can suddenly shift our trajectory in positive ways. Just as a lucky dice roll in Monopoly can change the dynamics of the game, seizing a sudden opportunity can dramatically enhance our life's journey. These advantageous events remind us to stay alert and ready to capitalize on the opportunities that come our way.

We may face obstacles that knock us back, but these moments are balanced with victories that elevate us higher. Every step builds on the previous one, ultimately helping us reach the game's end goal and complete our journey. Despite the challenges, the joy comes from how we handle these ups and downs, remaining resilient and continuing to progress toward our dreams, even if the path isn't straightforward. Eventually, like reaching the final square in Chutes and Ladders or building a property empire in Monopoly, we will get to our destination.

We can't predict every twist and turn, especially when it comes to people we meet or sudden opportunities that come our way. Life has a knack for bringing the right people into our lives exactly when we need them, often in ways we never saw coming. These moments can lead to substantial changes, pushing us toward paths we hadn't thought about before. This unpredictability isn't something to be scared of. Instead, it's part of life to welcome, bringing growth and experiences we might otherwise miss.

When facing life's unpredictable nature, taking a moment to pause is really valuable. Knowing when to step back, think things over, and wait for clearer understanding can turn a tricky situation into a chance to reflect and realign our paths.

Think about playing a game and encountering a setback that makes you slide backward or disrupts your plan. In the game, we have to play by the rules and keep going. But in life, we can choose to pause, take a break, and think about our next move. This pause isn't about quitting or leaving the game. It's about giving ourselves a chance to rethink and choose a direction that better matches what we really want.

By welcoming the chance to pause during life's journey, we give ourselves a moment to reset. This lets us look past the immediate hurdles and see the bigger picture of where we're headed. Having this broader view is crucial for moving forward thoughtfully and with purpose, making sure our actions lead us toward a life that's not just successful on the outside but also rewarding and fulfilling.

Concentrating on the next step allows us to deal with uncertainty. It's like walking through fog with a lantern that shows just a few steps ahead, enough to keep moving.

Hitting pause can sometimes be the best action we take, especially when life throws us a curveball. Take Tom's story, for instance. Faced with a career hurdle, he chose to step back and listen softly instead of rushing to find a solution. He spent time in nature, allowing the natural world's calm and beauty to give him space for thought. This was about more than taking a break. It was a deliberate choice to seek clarity.

In the stillness of nature, away from the noise and demands of everyday life, Tom found the breathing room he needed. It's in these moments of quiet and reflection that we often see our path with new eyes. For Tom, this time was about more than escaping a setback. It was an opportunity to deeply consider what he truly wanted from his career and life.

This pause allowed Tom to align his career with his passions. The answers he found weren't forced or rushed. They emerged naturally with an unclouded vision of where he wanted to go next. This wasn't a simple decision about job titles or roles but about clarifying his personal values and aspirations.

Sometimes, the best way forward is to stop, reflect, and let our next steps reveal themselves. In doing so, we ensure that our actions are not just reactions to immediate challenges but steps toward a life that resonates with our deepest interests and joys.

We often find wisdom when we're not actively seeking answers, reminding us to take life one step at a time.

As we observe teens through their growth, we learn to appreciate the unknown. Just like spotting the hidden image in a Magic Eye™, the real beauty of this journey is revealed through wisdom, curiosity, and seeing how all our moments are connected.

· · ·

Harmony in the Family Beat

Raising teens is like being in a busy, noisy city. Sometimes, it feels like everything's moving too fast, and it's hard to keep up. Teens can be tough, with their eye rolls, wanting to be alone, or not talking much. Parents can get really worried. But even when things feel super crazy, there's a way to make things calmer. It's called the Inner Connection Quest.

This quest is different from other programs because it doesn't just look at what's happening on the outside. It helps change how you deal with your thoughts and feelings. This way, you can find peace no matter how wild things get. Together, we can create a family life that's all about getting along, understanding each other, and making good memories. This can happen even when teens are having a tough time.

The journey begins by taking a moment to step back. We're often so overwhelmed by the constant buzz around us that we lose touch with our inner voice. While it's true that we can't control every thought that pops into our head, we hold the reins when it comes to deciding which thoughts deserve our attention.

Picture our thoughts as leaves gently drifting along the surface of a river. We have the choice to watch them glide by, resisting the urge to grasp at them. When we choose to engage with certain thoughts, we breathe life into them. That transforms them into emotions. It's similar to how we can become fully absorbed in the experience of watching a 3D movie, feeling every scene as though it were unfolding right before our eyes. Similarly, our thoughts wield the power to stir emotions within us. They prompt reactions as though these thoughts were playing out in real life.

This act of letting thoughts pass without engagement allows us to clear our heads. In this newfound clarity, we gain perspective. Many of our worries are about things beyond our control or are not as serious as they seemed in the heat of the moment. This understanding that we can choose our focus and reaction can bring a sense of peace.

In this fast-paced world, where digital screens often demand our attention, offering someone our undivided focus is a precious gift. It fosters a deeper connection and creates memorable moments. Being wholeheartedly present with each other builds stronger, more meaningful relationships. Ordinary interactions can turn into cherished memories that last a lifetime.

It's okay to talk about how we feel, even when it feels a bit scary. Sharing what's worrying us or what we're not sure about can help everyone feel a bit better. It shows that being open is okay and that we all go through tough times.

This journey is something we do together with our teens. It's about us all working together to create a family life that feels right for everyone. This means finding the perfect balance between guiding them and letting them discover things on their own. It's about building a family that feels like a supportive team, where everyone knows they are loved and supported.

The Inner Connection Quest is all about ensuring that our family can find a way to share beautiful moments together, even when life gets really busy and wild. This includes understanding each other, feeling close, and making happy memories.

Seeing With New Eyes

Imagine seeing everything with fresh eyes, like the wonder in a baby's gaze or the excitement of a first date. Achieving this in our daily lives and relationships means letting go of old views and being open to the joy and wonder around us. It's about appreciating life without trying to label or understand everything immediately.

The key is to hold on to the good feelings. Think of it like enjoying a beautiful sunset without trying to figure out all the colors in the sky. Just feel the beauty and be thankful for it. Gratitude makes us happier, and although there might seem to be many reasons to be unhappy, a clear mind can change our entire outlook. A peaceful mind is a little bit of heaven right here on Earth.

When we approach people and situations with curiosity and kindness, we see them in a new light. We learn and grow from each interaction instead of just going through the motions, keeping our relationships fresh and exciting.

When things get challenging or confusing, we can take a moment to feel what's going on inside us instead of reacting right away. We can ask, "What is this feeling trying to show me?" This pause can lead to understanding and new insights, showing us a way forward that we hadn't seen before.

By doing this, the happy feelings come back naturally. We find joy not because the world has changed but because we've chosen to see it differently. We start to appreciate the trivial things in life more, making every day and every interaction richer and more meaningful.

This insight sheds light on valuable lessons that guide us through life's winding paths. Life is comparable to a board game with unexpected surprises. This journey teaches us to keep going until we find joy, even when things get tough. Appreciating new friends and chances that come our way is valuable, as they can change our path for the better.

Taking time to think and see things clearly when we're unsure is really helpful, similar to how Tom found peace and innovative ideas by spending time in nature. These quiet moments are good for us to figure out what we genuinely want to do. They can help us think about our lives and align our steps with what matters to us. By keeping these lessons in mind, we can make our journey through life not just about reaching goals but also about being deeply satisfied and happy with where we are.

Seeing life in a new way, being thankful for the small things, and enjoying every day can transform how we experience each day. These habits prompt us to think about the overlooked joys in our routine and how we can feel more joy through our daily actions. It also shows us how much the people we meet and the things we do can influence our path. By staying open to what comes our way and cherishing the people around us, we can have a life that's not only successful but also happy and meaningful.

In times when we feel overwhelmed, frustrated, or upset, we can ask, "How can I take a pause to help me see my path more clearly, and what new perspectives can I gain from this?"

At the end of each day, we can ask ourselves, "What simple moments today brought me joy, and how do they connect to the larger journey of my life?"

The scene with the musician playing in a busy place tells us that even when life is full and noisy, we can still find a special tune in the simple joys we encounter. This tune is what the Inner Connection Quest is all about. It encourages us to stop for a moment, listen softly, and see how our lives are woven together with others. It reminds us that finding our true selves and feeling content isn't only about the things we do on our own. It's also about the stories we share and our connections with people around us.

Next up, we're heading into a chapter called "Sunset Reflections." We'll share stories and thoughts on how quiet moments help us understand ourselves better and feel closer to everything around us.

SUNSET REFLECTIONS

I STARTED A PRACTICE DURING MY HIGH SCHOOL YEARS. A simple assignment to observe sunsets for a couple of months had evolved into a meaningful ritual that influenced my perspective on life. Each evening, as if pulled by an unseen force, I found myself on the porch, spellbound by the sun's glorious descent.

This serene activity became my haven from life's chaos. With its vivid colors, every sunset seemed to outshine the last, enveloping me in a celestial display of beauty. In these moments, I felt as if each sunset was the universe's personal serenade to me.

The memories of those past sunsets still resonate within me. The depth of our connections extends beyond human interaction, encompassing the natural world and the cosmos. This peaceful backdrop perfectly introduces a discussion about innerconnectedness. Although it's a broad topic, let's delve into it, even for a moment.

Think back to times when you've felt connected with people, nature, or something bigger than us all. Was it staring at a breathtaking landscape or experiencing a moment of spiritual clarity? These are glimpses into how everything in our lives is connected.

They show the deep ties we share with others, the world around us, and a greater energy. Reflecting on these moments helps us see the vast web of life and our place in it.

The Mosaic of Universal Values

Imagine a world where kindness, understanding, and looking out for each other are the guiding principles. This is the essence of the mosaic of universal values, a vibrant blend of respect, empathy, and compassion that unites us all. Visualize the Pattersons, a family that loves to gather around their dinner table filled with delicious dishes. It's not just about the food. It's about the love and joy that flows freely. This warmth and care at the family table is a tiny reflection of the big picture of how we should treat each other in society. It shows us that kindness and understanding can make any place feel like home.

Now, let's take a trip around the world to see this mosaic in action. In Japan, there's a wonderful way of treating guests called "omotenashi." It's all about making people feel special through anticipation, selflessness, and sincerity. Imagine planning the perfect visit for a friend, thinking about every little detail to make them happy. That's "omotenashi," which is like a masterclass in kindness and making every moment count.

If we journey to Africa, we find "Ubuntu," a powerful idea that means "I am because we are." It's about feeling connected to everyone and understanding that we're all part of a big family. Ubuntu teaches us that our happiness is linked with others' happiness. It's a reminder that sharing a smile or helping a neighbor makes our world a better place.

In Hawaii, the concept of "Aloha" embodies much more than just a warm greeting. It's a way of life rooted in love, peace, and compassion, bringing people together like a close-knit family. Aloha is all about sharing joy, respecting others, and fostering kindness in every interaction. Imagine inviting someone into your home and treating them like family, making them feel comfortable, appreciated, and at ease.

In South Asia, the concept of "Seva" (selfless service) in Hinduism and Sikhism emphasizes kindness without expecting anything in return. Seva often manifests as providing free meals in temples or volunteering to help those in need. This tradition teaches that helping others is not only a noble act but also a means of finding spiritual fulfillment and purpose.

In New Zealand, the Māori concept of Manaakitanga promotes hospitality, kindness, and respect. It calls for treating guests and strangers with the utmost care, ensuring their well-being and comfort. This generosity reflects positively on the host, whose reputation is shaped by the way they treat others. Whether welcoming friends or strangers, Manaakitanga emphasizes sharing resources, offering guidance, and maintaining harmony, making visitors feel valued and deeply connected to the community.

These traditions from around the globe show us how universal values of kindness, empathy, and compassion weave together to create a colorful and vibrant mosaic of human experience. Like a masterpiece that gets its beauty from every brushstroke, our world becomes more beautiful with every act of kindness and every gesture of heart.

This big, beautiful picture tells us that although we're all different, we share the same hopes and dreams. These values are like a language everyone understands, a bridge that brings us all closer, no matter where we are. It's a reminder that every thread, color, and pattern is important in the great mosaic of life and makes the picture complete.

. . .

Finding Harmony in Life's Journey

Think of our lives as threads in a vast community mosaic, tied together by shared values. It's like feeling the calm at sunset, a time to think about all we've learned and grown. Sunsets are special. They're like nature's way of showing us life's beauty, with each color telling its own story.

During these quiet times, we can listen softly and see how our stories are part of a much bigger picture. Our experiences and the values we hold dear make our lives fuller and more colorful. These sunset reflections help blur the lines between us and the rest of the world. We're all connected. This feeling frees us to be who we are, have influence, and live in harmony with everything around us.

How do our personal journeys weave into the larger fabric of life? How do we, as individuals, strengthen the communities we're part of? Reflecting on these kinds of questions helps us appreciate our unique role in the world. Understanding this connection brings us a deep sense of purpose.

After these reflections, we feel more aware of our place in the world and ready for what's next. Just as the sunset leads to night and then a new morning, our thoughts and realizations get us set for another day. Life goes in cycles, just like this.

With every new day, we have a chance to use what we've learned, to start fresh with a clearer view of our visions. The insights from our quiet times prepare us to take on each day with more meaning and a stronger desire to help our community and the planet.

This cycle of thinking, learning, and starting again can keep our personal growth alive and our influence beneficial. By continuously reflecting, learning, and beginning anew, we keep moving forward, ready to meet new challenges, grow, and add our unique thread to the mosaic of life.

. . .

Resolving Conflicts Through Connection

At the heart of our story of being deeply connected, the family can stand out as a key player. It's where lofty ideas like respect, empathy, and compassion are not just talked about but can be felt and practiced. These values can light up family life, showing up in everyday routines, chats, and yes, even in the disagreements we face.

Picture a cozy living room, buzzing with the day's stories and filled with the smells of dinner cooking. Here, respect is essential, but it's shown in actions, not just words. It's part of the family's everyday ways. Even when family members don't agree entirely, these moments aren't just hurdles. They're chances to come together stronger with more understanding.

In this family warmth, different opinions aren't causes for fights but chances to grow closer and know each other better. Everyone gets to speak their mind, and all viewpoints matter. Potential clashes can turn into opportunities for bonding.

Take the Pattersons' living room as an example. It's set up not just for kicking back but to invite simple conversations. The comfortable seats encourage open chats, and the gentle lighting makes everyone feel at ease. Even a simple nod or a reassuring pat on the back here says, "We get it, let's work through this together." It's a place where even misunderstandings become moments that bring them closer.

The teen years are a time of searching and figuring out personal identity. And it's when a family can offer a steady base of support and acceptance. These years laid the groundwork for a lifetime of understanding what really matters and how we connect with others.

The values nurtured in the family spread everywhere, helping to weave a community that's all about sticking together. From simple family meals to involvement in local happenings, these actions pump life and vibrancy into our shared human journey.

Think back to times when you've seen strong family ties. As we explore these connections, let's listen closely to nurture bonds that can transform our families and positively impact the community. These reflections give us insight into how family dynamics work and show the significant influence family bonds have on personal growth and the broader society.

Interwoven Worlds

In our lives, the way we feel, think, and act is all connected, like a web. Our emotions paint our experiences, while our intellect helps us navigate through them. And then there's our will, which is about choosing how to respond to those feelings and thoughts. Imagine this as a journey where our feelings, ideas, and decisions all walk together, shaping who we are and what we do.

Understanding this journey helps us see that we're not just a bunch of random parts but a whole person. Think about how this plays out in a family. Beyond the everyday stuff, like what's for dinner or whose turn it is to do the dishes, there's something bigger going on. It's about the values and beliefs that guide us, shaped by our experiences and what we learn along the way. These values are like a compass, helping us navigate life, especially when things get tough.

Take the Patterson family, for example. They love exploring diverse cultures right in their own city. Every festival and event was an adventure. It was a chance to connect their own experiences with the broader world.

At a Diwali festival, the stories of light overcoming darkness resonated with the Pattersons' own challenges and victories. It was more than just a celebration, as it showcased resilience and hope, reflecting the family's belief in staying positive through difficult times.

During a Japanese tea ceremony, the calm and precision of the ritual taught them about mindfulness and the beauty of simplicity. It offered them a moment to pause and reflect on the importance of respect and patience, lessons they could naturally apply in their daily lives.

At a Brazilian carnival, the joy and vibrancy of the music and dance filled them with a sense of life's spontaneity. It was a vivid reminder to enjoy life and embrace the moment, inspiring the family to treasure their time together and create joyful occasions.

Through these experiences, the Pattersons didn't just learn about other cultures. They deepened their understanding of themselves. Seeing how their own values fit into a bigger picture strengthened their sense of belonging and meaning. Each event, with its unique traditions, provided them with opportunities to grow, learn, and connect on a deeper level.

This journey into diverse cultures reflected more than just their values. It enriched them, offered new insights, affirmed their emotions, and expanded their view of the world. Whether it was finding common ground in stories of resilience, appreciating the depth of traditions, or celebrating the joy of life, each experience brought them closer to understanding their place in the world and the beauty of being part of a diverse human family.

The Unseen Webs of Inner Value

In a village on the edge of a bustling city, something extraordinary was about to happen: an elephant, a creature the villagers had never seen before, was coming. Excitement filled the air. Among the crowd were those who were blind and had lived in a world without light, using their other senses to understand their surroundings. When the elephant finally arrived, its sheer size was astonishing, but even more remarkable were the stories it seemed to carry.

The villagers who could see marveled at the elephant's immense presence, while those who couldn't see touched the animal to understand its form. Each person felt a different part: the rough skin, the sharp tusk, the swaying tail. This story, known to many, usually highlights how our perceptions can be limited. But let's view it from another angle, focusing on something deeper: our inner value.

Think of the elephant as representing our life experiences, skills, setbacks, and dreams. We are like the villagers, each trying to understand our worth but often seeing only a tiny fragment of the bigger picture.

For instance, one villager, feeling the elephant's side, might think of it as a broad wall, much like how we sometimes define ourselves by one significant event or trait. A failure may seem like an unyielding wall blocking our progress.

Another villager, holding the tail, might believe it's a rope, similar to how a particular talent or interest makes us feel special. But just as the tail isn't the whole elephant, one skill doesn't sum up our entire worth.

A third villager, touching the elephant's tusk, could believe it's a spear, just as a sharp challenge might seem like the only thing shaping us. Meanwhile, the villager holding the trunk might perceive it as a snake, representing how unpredictable events twist and turn in our lives.

Our value is like the elephant itself: complex and composed of many parts. It's the combination of our experiences that shapes us. A setback in one area can lead to growth in another, and unexpected challenges can reveal hidden strengths.

The elephant's footprints symbolize the subtle yet meaningful impact of our life experiences. Just as the villagers share their observations of the elephant to gain a complete understanding, teens can gain clarity by sharing and reflecting on their own journeys. These footprints represent the small, often overlooked moments that shape who we are, whether it's a conversation with a friend, a challenging class, or trying out a new activity.

Like the villagers sharing stories to piece together the elephant's full picture, teens often miss the bigger picture in their own lives. By valuing these small, unnoticed moments and connections, they can see how everything links together to reveal the depth and richness of their experiences. Recognizing these subtle but significant moments leads to a deeper understanding of themselves and their role in society.

Following this trail of quiet footprints can guide teens on a journey of discovery that ultimately uncovers the intricate tapestry of their lives. Understanding the elephant by following its tracks means observing the patterns, paths, and imprints it leaves behind. By studying these footprints, we learn about the elephant's movements, habits, and behaviors, ultimately providing a clearer understanding of the animal as a whole.

The tracks reveal where the elephant has traveled, its preferred paths, and how it navigates various terrains. These tracks symbolize our own life journeys, showing the routes we've taken, the challenges we've faced, and the choices that have shaped us.

The size and depth of the footprints reflect the elephant's size and weight, much like our actions and experiences leave impressions that illustrate the magnitude of our challenges and achievements.

The presence of other tracks indicates a group or family moving together, representing how relationships and connections influence our paths.

By following these tracks, we can piece together a comprehensive picture of the elephant, just as reflecting on our own past experiences helps us understand ourselves more deeply. Recognizing the "footprints" of our actions, relationships, and decisions reveals patterns and behaviors that lead to self-discovery and personal growth.

Finding Calm in the Storm

Viewing the elephant's footprints as a metaphor for our family journey sheds light on how we can ease tension at home by deeply connecting with ourselves. Many believe that resolving family issues, particularly bridging the gap between parents and teens, requires external help. But often, the solution is more straightforward and closer to home.

Parenting through the teen years can feel like navigating a storm. These challenging moments are when connecting with our inner wisdom matters most. This Inner Connection Quest isn't about seeking advice to change our teens. It's about looking within ourselves to recognize and change how we react and feel.

Just like a captain uses the stars for navigation, we can listen to our inner wisdom. Our thoughts can guide us or create confusion if followed without reflection. By observing our thoughts without being overwhelmed by them, we can decide which deserves our attention. This careful selection helps us approach family situations with greater peace and clarity.

Choosing to connect more with ourselves doesn't mean ignoring the difficulties of raising teenagers. Instead, it equips us to face these challenges with a calm mind and clear insight. Deep down, we all possess a wise part of ourselves. The key is to pause and listen carefully for answers to what's happening in our families.

In this process, we learn to ease our worries, whether they come from self-doubt, questioning our value, or uncertainty about the best way to handle a situation. Tapping into the wisdom within us will guide us forward.

Garden of Growth and Unity

With her nurturing spirit as a nurse, Joyce Patterson was the heartbeat of her family's daily rhythm. After hours of providing strength and comfort to those in need, she'd return home to her sanctuary, letting the day's weight melt away at the door.

She had her special rituals: 'sunset reflections' in the evening, sifting through the day's events, and 'dawn awakenings' in the morning, welcoming each day with intention and hope. These moments weren't just pauses but served as bridges over troubled waters, offering clarity and renewal.

Despite the love in the Patterson home, it wasn't immune to conflict and the silent struggles of growing up. Jarad was caught in the whirlwind of his work, and their children, Ann and Jake, each wrestled with the trials of youth, drifting in their own currents and struggling to find their place in the family.

In her quiet moments of reflection, Joyce noticed threads of disconnection weaving through her family. Ann's silence and Jake's search for belonging set off alarms in her heart. She pondered deeply on how to bring them closer, to be their lighthouse in the fog.

One evening, as dusk fell and the sky blushed, Joyce had an idea as bright as the stars: a community garden. This was about more than planting seeds. It was about planting hope, a way for the family to grow together and understand one another better.

Though the idea sprouted with mixed feelings, it slowly took root. Ann's green thumb and Jake's tech skills found common ground in their new project, and as the garden flourished, so did the Pattersons. They found laughter, lessons, and love among the blooms and bees. Ann discovered her strength beyond books, and Jake realized his worth in every watered seedling.

The garden was more than just a patch of earth. It became a canvas of connection for the Pattersons and their neighbors. It reminded them that prosperity blooms brightest when nurtured by community care and kindness.

Through dirt and growth, the Pattersons created a story of inner connection, turning a simple idea into a living proof of the beauty of working together. This chapter sheds light on our Inner Connection Quest, showing that watching sunsets helps us see life's beauty and feel closer to the universe while listening softly lets us find joy and calmness in our own hearts.

The story of the Patterson family adds another layer to this quest. Through their acts of kindness, sitting together in their living room, and working in the garden, they teach us the joy that comes from sharing and caring for each other. These aren't just activities or service projects. They're opportunities to weave stronger bonds with our families and neighbors, making everyone feel included and important. It's a reminder that when we join hands and hearts in small projects or simply by being there for each other, we build a happier and more connected community.

The elephant story in this chapter isn't just about viewing things from different angles. It's an exploration of recognizing our own worth and the unique value of others. It's a playful yet profound lesson that each of us is a vital piece of the bigger picture of life. This story encourages us to listen, share, and appreciate the diverse experiences and perspectives that enrich our journey together.

Forming a habit of watching sunsets becomes something truly special, like finding a little magic each day. Do you have a small daily ritual that makes your day better, lifting your mood and changing your perspective?

In relation to the Inner Connection Quest, this chapter teaches us to find peace and joy in nature, value our relationships, and embrace the richness of human experience. By exploring these themes, we learn to live more fully with open hearts, appreciating the world's beauty and the power of kindness. This leads to a deeper understanding of ourselves and the connections that unite us all.

Prepare for "The Journey to Balance," where we explore Anthony's story. This next chapter promises a heartwarming adventure. Join us to see how Anthony's journey unfolds and find a little inspiration to seek balance in our active lives.

THE JOURNEY TO BALANCE

ANTHONY'S WORLD WAS A BLUR. EACH DAY WAS A MARATHON of tasks and achievements. From the moment the alarm clock pierced the morning silence, it was a sprint through homework, soccer practice, student meetings, and the endless stream of deadlines that defined high school life. To outsiders, Anthony was the epitome of success in productivity and ambition. But beneath the surface, fatigue had begun to erode the thrill of accomplishment, leaving a sense of emptiness in its wake.

One evening, Anthony's parents, Maria and David, observed their child hunching over a textbook. The glow of the laptop cast shadows across tired eyes. The scene was all too familiar, yet tonight, something within them stirred. The relentless pace they'd once admired was now consuming their child.

Maria broke the silence. Her voice was soft. "Anthony, you're always on the go. When was the last time you just... stopped for a minute?"

Anthony's fingers paused mid-type, the question hanging in the air like an unfamiliar melody. "I can't stop, Mom. There's always something I need to do." The words had propelled Anthony forward but now seemed to echo back with a hollow ring.

David leaned forward. "But at what cost? We've noticed you're not yourself lately. It's time for a change of pace."

Anthony looked up. "What are you thinking about?"

Maria exchanged a glance with David. "A family camping trip. No schedules, no goals. Just us and the river."

Anthony scoffed. "The river? What's that going to solve?"

David replied. " You'd be surprised how nice it is when you're just out there, taking it easy."

And so, the plans were set in motion.

The Misstep of Constant Motion

The morning air was crisp, a gentle mist rising from the Great River as the Rodriguez family unpacked their gear. The serene beauty of the riverbank, with its chorus of chirping birds and the soft murmur of flowing water, set a tranquil backdrop vastly different from the hectic rhythm of their daily lives.

Maria, who had been watching the river's gentle flow, turned to Anthony. "We could just sit by the river. Watch how it flows; listen to the sounds." Her suggestion floated in the air.

Anthony's response came quickly. "We're here to do things, aren't we?"

The day unfolded in a flurry of action. They kayaked through the brisk waters of the Great River, hiked up one of the neighboring hills, and fished as the sun dipped below the horizon. Each activity was tackled with a relentless drive, leaving little room for rest or reflection.

As the day wore on, the physical toll of the non-stop activities began to manifest. Anthony's steps grew slower. Sitting by the campfire that evening, Maria asked, "Anthony, today was fun, but it felt like we were racing against the clock. Is that really how we want to spend our time here?"

"Sure, we never do this kind of stuff. I'm tired now. Thanks for today."

The dawn of the second day by the Great River greeted the Rodriguez family with a chorus of birds and a gentle breeze rustling through the trees. Despite the previous day's exhaustion, Anthony woke with a renewed determination to explore further. The beauty of the surrounding nature seemed like an endless canvas, waiting to be filled with strokes of adventure.

The family set out on a hike. As they navigated a particularly rocky stretch, Anthony's foot found an uneven patch of ground, twisting awkwardly—a sharp pain shot through his ankle. The fall was sudden. Anthony sat on the path. Frustration and pain mingled in equal measure.

"This is ridiculous," Anthony cried.

The hike back to their campsite was slow, and Anthony leaned on David for support. Each step reminded him of his limit. The twisted ankle forced Anthony into a stillness that had been avoided at all costs.

Back at camp, with Anthony's ankle wrapped and elevated, the family settled into an unplanned quiet time. Anthony lay back. The pain in his ankle was only a dull ache now, but he was bothered by a swirl of thoughts and emotions.

Embracing the Flow

Confined to a chair by the river's edge, Anthony's world slowed down to the rhythm of the natural world. The initial stirrings of frustration and impatience gradually gave way to a sense of calm acceptance. Surrounded by the serene beauty of the river and the forest, Anthony began to watch, listen softly, and see for the first time.

The river flowed endlessly, yet it possessed a peaceful assurance in its journey. The dance of light on the water, the gentle rustling of leaves in the breeze, and the occasional splash of fish jumping created a symphony of nature that was both vibrant and soothing.

"It's beautiful, isn't it?" Anthony murmured, in awe, to no one in particular. The statement was more an expression of inner realization than a question seeking affirmation.

David, who had been setting up a fishing rod, paused and sat beside Anthony, sharing the view. "It's always been here, Anthony. Sometimes, we need to be still to notice the beauty that surrounds us."

As these words settled in, Anthony felt a shift in perspective. The river, with its effortless flow and boundless energy, seemed to offer unconditional love. It flowed without asking for anything in return, nurturing life along its banks, giving itself freely to all who sought comfort and nourishment.

This realization sparked a cascade of thoughts. The river did not discriminate. It did not withhold its bounty based on the actions or merits of those it supported. It simply was. It gave, supported, and loved without condition. Anthony felt and knew this was the essence of true love, a love that asks for nothing in return but exists to enrich and embrace.

The day unfolded with Anthony lost in contemplation, the will to do and achieve momentarily forgotten. Instead, there was an inner connection to the present moment, to the beauty and love offered so freely by nature. Sensing the shift in their teen, Anthony's family joined in this space of quiet reflection, their presence a comforting constant.

As the sun began its descent, Anthony shared this newfound insight. "I never realized how much love there is around us, in everything. The river, the trees, and the sun don't need us to do anything to deserve their beauty. They are always just there."

David nodded. "Nature has a way of teaching us what's important. It's a love that's always there, even when we're too caught up in our own worlds to notice it."

As the family sat together that evening, watching the stars emerge in the clear night sky, there was a shared sense of peace and gratitude. For Anthony, the insight into unconditional love offered by nature was transformative. It wasn't about the successes or the awards but about being a part of the world's natural flow.

This day of forced stillness by the river became a turning point for Anthony, a lesson in the power of being present and the beauty of receiving and giving love without conditions.

A New Rhythm Emerges

Things were different when Anthony and his parents returned from their trip by the Great River. Anthony wasn't just rushing from one task to another anymore. There was a new way of doing things, mixing demanding work with moments to enjoy life.

Everyone could see the change in Anthony. School and sports were still important, but now there was time to stop and look around, to thoroughly take in what was happening.

One night, while they were all sitting around the dinner table, Anthony shared what was on his mind. "I think I get it now. It's not just about being busy all the time. That trip, being by the river, it showed me how to enjoy life."

Anthony started doing things differently after that. There was time for homework and sports, but also moments for quiet and for enjoying the small things. Friends noticed Anthony was more there when they spent time together, simply listening and sharing. Even teachers saw a deeper side to Anthony's answers and thoughts in class.

It wasn't always easy. Sometimes, old habits of rushing around came back, and the pressure to keep achieving was intense. But remembering the river and its calm flow helped Anthony remember to balance arduous work with being sensitive to the love of his family and the beauty of the world.

As life went on, Anthony kept up with goals, but now he appreciated the things he had, the people he knew, and the joy he felt. This made life richer and more impressive than before. The drive to accomplish was still there, but now it was mixed with the zest of being alive.

Paddling and Floating

Imagine life as a vast, flowing river. This river, filled with twists and turns, represents the journey we're all on. Now, think of "doing" and "being" as two essential ways to navigate this river, each affecting how we feel and our overall happiness in different but equally important ways.

Doing is like paddling your boat. It's all about action, moving forward, achieving goals, and tackling challenges head-on. When we're in "doing" mode, we feel a rush of accomplishment and pride as we reach each milestone or destination. But, just like paddling non-stop can tire us out, being in constant motion can lead to stress and exhaustion if we don't take breaks to rest, listen softly, and enjoy the scenery.

Being is like letting your boat float along with the current. It's about being present and fully immersing yourself in the here and now without worrying about the next rapid or bend in the river. This state encourages us to embrace our thoughts and feelings as they are, without judgment. It brings a sense of peace and contentment, allowing us to recharge and appreciate the beauty of our journey.

Navigating the river of life requires a balance between paddling and floating, doing and being. Leaning too heavily on one can either leave us exhausted or stuck in place. It's about finding the right rhythm that keeps us moving forward but also allows us to enjoy the journey.

Now, let's bring our boat's crew into the picture: emotion, intellect, and will. These three are key in helping us steer through life's waters, balancing our efforts to do and our moments to just be.

Emotions are like the wind. Sometimes, they're a gentle breeze that nudges us forward. Other times, they become a gusty storm that churns the water around us. They can fuel our journey with passion or caution us with fear. Like seasoned sailors, we learn to read the winds of our emotions, knowing when to set sail and when to anchor down and wait out the storm. Our emotions add color and texture to our journey, influencing how we see and experience the world.

Our intellect is the map and compass of our journey, guiding us through the river's twists and turns. It helps us plot our course, tackle challenges, and reflect on the path we've traveled. In moments of action, our intellect shines, plotting the best route forward. In moments of stillness, it enriches our journey, allowing us to ponder the mysteries beneath the surface and the beauty surrounding us.

Will is the strength to steer and adjust the sails, deciding when to push forward and when to glide with the current. It's our ability to make deliberate choices, harnessing the winds of emotion and using the guidance of our intellect. Will keeps us balanced, ensuring we move toward our goals while staying true to ourselves and savoring the journey.

The delicate dance between doing and being, guided by our emotions, intellect, and will, is about using our understanding and feelings to navigate life. We can decide when to act and when to pause, which allows us to fully experience and appreciate the beauty of the journey. This balance makes our voyage not just about reaching destinations but about finding joy and fulfillment in the journey itself.

In the grand adventure down life's river, there's a secret that seasoned navigators know well. The power of "being" often unlocks the deepest insights and wisdom. While the thrill of paddling, of conquering rapid after rapid, has its place, it's in the quiet moments of floating that we can listen softly to the river's song. It's when we let go of the oars and allow ourselves to be carried by the current that we notice the patterns in the water, the way the light dances off the waves, and the subtle guidance of the river's flow.

These moments of stillness invite reflection and a deeper understanding of ourselves and the journey ahead. They remind us that sometimes, by doing less, we gain more clarity and a renewed sense of direction. So, while the rhythm of "doing" propels us forward, it's in the art of "being" that we find the wisdom to navigate life's river with grace and purpose.

Love, Insight, and Healing

Anita Moorjani's fight against cancer and her remarkable recovery is a story about healing and change.[1] She didn't just face the tough parts of her sickness. She also dealt with the challenging emotions and thoughts that came with it.

During her hardest days, Anita was scared, felt down, and thought about quitting. Before her near-death experience, she often put what others thought ahead of her own needs. She was caught up in trying to make everyone else happy, which added to her stress.

During her near-death experience, Anita felt a massive sense of love and peace, so different from the fear and discomfort she had felt before. She realized wanting to live wasn't about being scared of dying. It was about choosing life from a place of love for herself and everyone around her.

This insight changed everything for Anita. She shared her story. I'll paraphrase it.

It's a beautiful way of looking at life, she explains, where we recognize that we are perfect and connected to something bigger, called the Source. Imagine every morning feeling that we are complete, exactly right, and never apart from this Source. This idea isn't about being full of ourselves. It's about seeing our true value just as we are.

Living this way means we deeply love ourselves. We feel okay and at peace with every part of who we are, and we're excited to follow our life's calling. This way of thinking frees us from worrying about living up to what others expect or think of us. We let our inner wisdom shine through, feeling supported by a kind force guiding us.

We no longer question if we are good enough or if we can trust our gut feelings. We don't wonder about our life's true purpose or if we're brave enough to make it happen. Being worried about seeming "too different" or "unrealistic" with our dreams goes away. There's nothing in the way of feeling all the love available to us and the pure happiness of just being alive.

Through Anita's eyes, we learn about our direct connection to unconditional love and the joy of simply being here, free from fear and filled with love. Anita was able to listen softly to what truly mattered. There is love, acceptance, and authenticity within all of us.

Anita Moorjani spread her message everywhere, touching the hearts of many and sparking transformative changes in the lives of those who heard her story. Her book, "Dying to Be Me," delves into her experiences and the lessons she learned, providing valuable insights for anyone seeking to live more authentically by understanding and integrating these fundamental aspects of being.

Riding Life's Waves

Think about a day when things don't go your way. Your teen

comes home looking super stressed, and suddenly, you're both caught in a big wave of emotions. If you jump right into that wave without thinking, you might both end up getting tossed around.

Have you heard the safety talk on airplanes about oxygen masks? It's a good lesson for life, too. We must secure our masks before we can help anyone else with theirs. This demonstrates that staying calm and collected is important if we want to be there for teens when they're having a tough time. It's like you can't help another person to breathe if you aren't breathing.

I love being around our grandkids. There is incredible joy in watching them interact freely and be themselves. However, one time, I got all in my head over ridiculously trivial circumstances. I was tired and frustrated. I probably dealt with a couple of kid tantrums that wore down my nerves.

Anyway, I said something, and then one of the grandkids did something, and then another person said something contradicting what I said. The point is, I don't remember the details, but I remember the feeling of losing it with my precious grandchildren.

I felt so miserable that I locked myself in a room while the others were left wondering what was wrong with me. I called someone I trusted, and we talked about the situation. My biggest comment was that I absolutely hated how I was feeling. During our conversation, I realized it was time to let go of my old way of thinking.

Before diving into the concept of "emoji poop," it's helpful to understand that our minds are constantly filled with a stream of thoughts, like a river that never stops flowing. In this mental river, we encounter a wide range of ideas and memories, some uplifting and positive, while others are troubling or uncomfortable. How we choose to react to these thoughts can greatly impact our emotions and behavior.

This is where the "emoji poop" idea comes in. Taking life too personally is like picking up and holding onto an imaginary emoji poop from this river of thoughts. By focusing on and internalizing negative thoughts, we end up carrying an unnecessary burden that weighs us down. Instead, we can practice letting these unpleasant thoughts drift by without becoming attached to them, choosing to focus on the ideas that lift us up instead. Would you rather hold onto the emoji poop or let it flow away down the river?

If we are aware of the effects of thoughts, we can steer our mindset toward the more enriching and rewarding choices. What we think affects our emotions. We don't want to be misguided by feelings that push us away from our hearts of unconditional love. It simply zaps us of our joy.

When frustration threatened to take hold of me again, I promptly addressed it, recognizing that clinging to rigid viewpoints or impatience wasn't worth the emotional turmoil it created. This resolve allowed me to let go of such moments more effortlessly over time. The joy I experienced in the company of my grandchildren far outweighed the discontent of dwelling on trivial issues. This discovery not only enhanced my capacity to cherish the time spent with my grandchildren but also led me to reflect on broader life lessons.

In this chapter, we explored different insights pertaining to heart-filled living. Anthony, like many, struggled to find a balance between constant activity and the simple act of being present. Anita Moorjani emphasizes the importance of infusing our lives with love and joy. Encouraging teens to strike a balance between pursuing their goals and taking time to enjoy life's simpler pleasures can lead to a richer, more contented life. Discussing Moorjani's insights on how genuine healing and understanding emerge from actions rooted in love and joy opens the door to meaningful conversations with teens about discovering what can bring them lasting well-being.

How can we help teens get along well with their feelings, make smart choices with their brains, and follow their hearts in a way that's true to who they are? This question makes us think about how teens can listen to their feelings to guide them, use their brains to decide what's best and use their determination to go after what holds meaning to them instead of blindly doing what they think they should.

Both Anthony's experience and Anita Moorjani's story show us how special it is to "just be" and to enjoy the moment without worrying about having to do something all the time. How can our family find more chances to have precious moments together? We can plan regular family fun times to help us enjoy the present, whether in nature or just hanging out together.

Helping teens understand their feelings, think things through, and pursue what they love gives them an impressive set of tools for a happy life. This is where the Inner Connection Quest comes in. It's all about listening softly to let moments of calm and insight happen. It's about making memories with our families. So, let's make sure to cherish these valuable times, turning each day into a chance for appreciation and discovery.

In addition, understanding Anita Moorjani's insights and Anthony's story can deeply enrich our lives. Their journeys underscore how moments of insight can open us to feeling unconditional love. This love has always been there but is often overlooked amidst our daily routines.

We can tap into this boundless love when we pause, reflect, and connect with our inner selves. It's a reminder that, beyond our activities and achievements, lies the joy of being alive and connected to each other and the universe. Embracing this perspective can shift how we view our lives and relationships, guiding us toward a more loving and fulfilling existence. So, as we embark on our Inner Connection Quest, let's listen softly and embrace the insights that lead us to experience unconditional love.

AFTERWORD

Have you ever had a moment when you suddenly saw things differently, and everything started improving? When we take a moment to quiet our minds and open up to the deeper wisdom inside us, we can start to improve our lives.

This book was a wonderful journey with you. Being a parent, especially to teens, isn't just about dealing with tough times on the outside. It's also about going on an inner adventure to connect with our feelings and with each other.

We've discussed numerous aspects of a parenting adventure, like seeing the good things teens bring, understanding how love changes as we all grow, and getting better at showing we care. Through the demanding times and momentous changes, we are getting wiser along the way.

The message we've been talking about is a vision of TRUE LOVE. It's being real and true, knowing the value of helping out and being part of the community.

We've delved into the following four aspects of the Inner Connection Quest.

Growth and Development

Embarking on the Inner Connection Quest, we begin by building on our strengths and quickly recognize how our choices impact our lives and those around us. This journey encourages us to embrace understanding, resilience, and authenticity. At its core, it's about quieting the noise in our minds so we can hear the gentle whispers of wisdom that guide both parents and teens toward what truly matters. By doing so, we strengthen our confidence. And find joy.

Wholesome Relationships

The Inner Connection Quest guides us toward more fulfilling and supportive relationships. Through this journey, we prioritize empathy and love as essential for nurturing strong connections. We find that meaningful relationships arise from genuinely caring for and understanding others. This process deepens our connections and enriches our life experience, revealing how focusing on healthy relationships brings greater joy and contentment. Strong interpersonal bonds play a crucial role in creating a well-rounded and joyful life.

Making a Difference

Engaging with causes that resonate deeply with us brings fulfillment. The Inner Connection Quest encourages us to listen attentively and recognize our unique abilities to make a positive difference. This journey reveals our value and uncovers paths for meaningful impact. It enlightens us, helping us to leave a mark on the world that aligns with our most heartfelt visions.

Innerconnectedness

This quest shows how our relationships and the support we offer each other are crucial for growth and improvement. We create a sense of harmony by weaving together essential qualities like truth, beauty, and goodness while tuning in to our emotions, thoughts, and intentions. Connecting with something greater than ourselves enhances our interactions and enriches our lives, celebrating the beauty of connection as we expand our hearts to embrace deeper and wider bonds.

The FROGS guide provides practical tools for strengthening connections with teens, helping us grow together.

- Flexibility encourages us to adapt and go with the flow, just like water. This helps us handle surprises and changes smoothly.
- Rapport means building a strong, trusting friendship. It's like being on the same team, even when we don't agree entirely on everything. This friendship is key to a strong connection.
- Outcome tells us to look at the big picture and not worry too much about trivial things. We encourage our teens to aim high and follow what they're enthusiastic about.
- Grounding is about keeping it real and honest when we talk. Sharing from the heart is what this is all about.
- Simple Conversations remind us that just talking can make a substantial difference. These chats can lead to momentous changes and help us get closer.

Together, these ideas can guide us as we help teens on their path, making sure we're there for them, understanding them better, and building a stronger family bond.

As we reach the end of this book, let's see parenting as an ongoing journey of growth and love. Picture a winding path where we face challenges, share joy, and experience all of life's ups and downs. By embracing our interconnectedness, we embark on a journey that rewards us with deeper insights into love and life.

If you haven't done so already, I highly recommend exploring the available tools and practical resources.[1] Visit https://www.upliftinge ducation.com/resources. Join our community or sign up for our email list, and let's continue this conversation.

Our shared journey, filled with encounters and insights, motivates us to create an uplifting, lasting impact. We move forward with open hearts, fostering unbreakable bonds of love and endless discovery, lighting the way for others to follow.

ACKNOWLEDGMENTS

I want to express my deepest gratitude to the following organizations and individuals who have supported and contributed to the creation of this book:

I am grateful to the Universal Peace Federation (UPF) for its unwavering commitment to fostering global peace and understanding. The UPF's initiatives and dedication to creating a world of peace through interfaith dialogue, leadership development, and humanitarian efforts have significantly influenced the development of this book. Their vision of peace and collaboration across diverse communities has been an inspiration in my research and writing process.

The core of this book drew inspiration from the philosophical and humanitarian outlook of Dr. Sun Myung Moon and Dr. Hak Ja Han Moon. Their lifelong dedication to fostering peace, unity, and improving the human condition has profoundly influenced its content and spirit. I am eternally thankful for their legacy, which continues to catalyze positive change globally, touching lives and communities in countless meaningful ways.

I extend my heartfelt appreciation to the Three Principles movement, founded by Sydney Banks, whose teachings on Mind, Consciousness, and Thought have influenced the perspectives shared in this book.

My heartfelt thanks go to my family and friends, who have been a constant source of encouragement and support throughout this writing process. Their love and understanding have sustained me through this journey.

Finally, I would like to express my appreciation to the readers who have chosen to read this book. I hope the insights and ideas presented here are helpful and inspiring to you.

Thank you all for your contributions and support.

NOTES

INTRODUCTION

1. The Universal Peace Federation (UPF) USA is a non-profit organization with General Consultative Status with the United Nations ECOSOC, dedicated to promoting peace through interdependence, mutual prosperity, and universally shared values. It provides educational programs for leaders across all sectors of society, focusing on building a global network of peacebuilders, strong families, interfaith leaders, and peace ambassadors, without engaging in political activities. https://us.upf.org/

1. JOURNEY OF GROWTH AND CONNECTION

1. Various studies support parental engagement's positive impact on teens' well-being and success. A few examples include:

"The Role of Parental Involvement in Adolescents' Academic Achievement Trajectories: A Person-Centered Approach" by Binhuan Wang, et al. (2020)

"Parental Involvement and Adolescent Well-Being: A Systematic Review" by Lauren B. Vollinger, et al. (2019)

"The Power of Parental Involvement: Evidence, Ideas, and Tools for Student Success" by Karen L. Mapp and Ilene Carver (2013)

2. David Key is an award-winning transformative coach, author, and speaker who specializes in helping individuals achieve personal and professional goals through a blend of NLP, hypnosis, and the Three Principles, aiming to transform lives and the world collectively. https://davidkey.com/

2. FROM BABY GIRL TO CEO

1. Research shows that healthy family relationships are linked to positive social and emotional outcomes for children, and the family plays a critical role in teaching children about ethical behavior and morality, while a balance between individual and collective goals is essential for the healthy functioning of society and individual well-being:

• Collins, W. A., Maccoby, E. E., Steinberg, L., Hetherington, E. M., & Bornstein, M. H. (2000). Contemporary research on parenting: The case for nature and nurture. American Psychologist, 55(2), 218–232. https://doi.org/10.1037/0003-066X.55.2.218

• Doherty, W. J. (1997). The intentional family: Simple rituals to strengthen family ties. Reading, MA: Addison-Wesley.

• Kohlberg, L. (1981). The philosophy of moral development: Moral stages and the idea of justice. HarperCollins Publishers.

• Parsons, T. (1955). The American family: Its relations to personality and to the social structure. In R. E. L. Faris (Ed.), Handbook of modern sociology (pp. 276–350). Rand McNally.

• Triandis, H. C. (1989). The self and social behavior in differing cultural contexts. Psychological Review, 96(3), 506–520. https://doi.org/10.1037/0033-295X.96.3.506

4. "I THOUGHT YOU FORGOT ABOUT ME"

1. The work of psychologists like Brené Brown, who has extensively studied vulnerability, courage, and authenticity, further underscores the importance of genuine connections. Brown's research suggests that embracing vulnerability and forming authentic connections with others is key to living a full, happy life.

Brown, Brené. Daring Greatly: How the Courage to Be Vulnerable Transforms the Way We Live, Love, Parent, and Lead. Gotham Books, 2012.

5. THE BASICS

1. These references delve into the intimate dynamics of the relationship between tennis legends, Venus and Serena Williams. Aman Mohamed's article from Sportskeeda captures some of the most heartwarming quotes the sisters have said about each other, offering a glimpse into their deep bond. In 'Who Are Venus and Serena Williams?' by James Buckley, readers are taken on a journey through the lives of these iconic sisters, chronicling their rise to stardom and the challenges they faced. Lastly, the film 'King Richard' listed on IMDb, centers on their father Richard Williams, portraying his determination and vision in shaping the careers of his prodigious daughters.

Mohamed, Aman. "Serena Williams and Venus Williams' Best Quotes about Each Other ." Sportskeeda, Sportskeeda, 12 Oct. 2022, www.sportskeeda.com/tennis/serena-williams-venus-williams-best-quotes.

Buckley, James. Who Are Venus and Serena Williams? Jove Publications, 2017.

"King Richard." IMDb, IMDb.com, 19 Nov. 2021, www.imdb.com/title/tt9620288/.

2. This study found that teens with solid relationships with their parents and peers reported were more likely to perform well academically and had stronger social support networks: McLean, K. C., & Breen, A. V. (2009). *Relationships as contexts for learning: Parents' and peers' support of autonomy and control and early adolescents' math and science outcomes.* Journal of Youth and Adolescence, 38(3), 369-382

3. Beverley Wilson Hayes, with over three decades in recovery and self-discovery initiatives, is internationally esteemed as a spiritual connector and educator. Her career, significantly shaped by her mentor Dr. Roger Mills and the teachings of Three Principles Psychology, has spanned diverse environments, from communities grappling with high crime rates to the corporate sphere. Prompted by the encouragement of Syd Banks, Beverley's life mission is to facilitate others in accessing their inherent wisdom and insight. This mission manifests in her engagement with individuals and groups, leading seminars, webinars, and mentorship, all underscored by a profound dedication to love and support. It was Beverley's eloquent discussion on the art of "listening softly" that sparked the inspiration for the title of this book.

6. BENEATH THE SURFACE

1. Dr. Jay N. Giedd is a prominent neuroscientist whose research has focused on adolescent brain development.

   Giedd, J. N. (2008). *The teen brain: Insights from neuroimaging. Journal of Adolescent Health,* 42(4), 335-343.

2. Blakemore's 2008 study in "Nature Reviews Neuroscience" investigates the transformations in the adolescent brain, emphasizing their impact on social cognition and behavior. The research suggests that these neural changes are crucial for understanding the complex social interactions typical of teenage years.

   Blakemore, S. J. (2008). *The social brain in adolescence.* Nature Reviews Neuroscience, 9(4), 267-277

3. Erik Erikson's theory on psychosocial development is foundational in developmental psychology, and his ideas on the challenges and transformations faced during adolescence are well-documented in his writings.

   Erikson, E. H. (1968). Identity: Youth and crisis. New York: Norton & Co.

4. Sydney Banks' "Three Principles: Mind, Consciousness, and Thought" refers to foundational tenets that elucidate the facets of human psychological experience, asserting that the entire range of human behavior and feeling states are created through these formless principles. Banks' insights into the nature of mind, consciousness, and thought have significantly impacted psychology and educa-

tion, promoting a perspective that our experiences and feelings are generated from within, by our thoughts. sydbanks.com

7. NURTURING AUTHENTIC LOVE

1. According to a study published in the Journal of Marriage and Family, married couples tend to have longer, healthier, and happier lives than unmarried individuals: Waite, L. J., & Gallagher, M. (2000). *The case for marriage: Why married people are happier, healthier, and better off financially.* New York: Broadway Books

2. Research has shown that teens of married parents are more likely to become successful and happy adults with stable marriages: Amato, P. R., & Booth, A. (2001). *The legacy of parents' marital discord: Consequences for children's marital quality.* Journal of Personality and Social Psychology, 81(4), 627-638

    Stable marriages may provide children with a supportive and nurturing environment, leading to physical, emotional, and cognitive development: Kelly, J. B., & Emery, R. E. (2003). *Children's adjustment following divorce: Risk and resilience perspectives.* Family Relations, 52(4), 352-362.

8. JOURNEY THROUGH THE MIST

1. Giedd (2004) examines the adolescent brain's evolution through structural magnetic resonance imaging.

    Giedd, J. N. (2004). Structural magnetic resonance imaging of the adolescent brain. *Annals of the New York Academy of Sciences, 1021(1),* 77-85.

    Steinberg (2008) offers a social neuroscience lens on adolescent risk-taking propensity.

    Steinberg, L. (2008). A social neuroscience perspective on adolescent risk-taking. *Developmental Review, 28(1),* 78-106.

    Spear (2000) delves into the adolescent brain's development and its corresponding age-specific behavioral expressions.

    Spear, L. P. (2000). The adolescent brain and age-related behavioral manifestations. *Neuroscience & Biobehavioral Reviews, 24(4),* 417-463.

    Casey et al. (2008) presents a comprehensive exploration of the neural underpinnings and characteristics of the adolescent brain.

    Casey, B. J., Jones, R. M., & Hare, T. A. (2008). The adolescent brain. *Annals of the New York Academy of Sciences, 1124(1),* 111-126.

9. ANCHORED IN UNDERCURRENTS

1. "Man's Search for Meaning" by Viktor Frankl is a profound psychological work that details the author's Holocaust experiences and introduces logotherapy, his theory that the fundamental human drive is a search for meaning in life.

    Frankl, Viktor E. "Man's Search for Meaning: An Introduction to Logotherapy." Beacon Press, originally published in 1946.

10. DIGITAL DIARY OF DYLAN

1. Kant's philosophy suggests that the moral value of our actions comes from performing our duty for its own sake, yet questions whether duty alone can fulfill our search for meaning. These ideas are broadly based on Immanuel Kant's ethical theory, particularly his works in "Groundwork of the Metaphysics of Morals."

11. LOVE AND COMMUNITY

1. Kernis, M. H., & Goldman, B. M. (2006). A multicomponent conceptualization of authenticity: Theory and research. In M. P. Zanna (Ed.), *Advances in experimental social psychology*, Vol. 38, pp. 283–357). Elsevier Academic Press. https://doi.org/10.1016/S0065-2601(06)38006-9

14. HARMONY IN THE HUSTLE

1. Abraham Maslow proposed the Hierarchy of Needs, a model that outlines the sequence of human motivations, starting from basic physiological needs and culminating in self-actualization. This theory suggests that individuals can pursue higher-level psychological needs only when basic needs are met.

    Maslow, A. H. (1943). A theory of human motivation. *Psychological Review,* 50(4), 370–396.

16. THE JOURNEY TO BALANCE

1. Anita Moorjani's remarkable journey from battling cancer to miraculous recovery exemplifies the power of healing and transformation.

    Moorjani, Anita. *Dying to Be Me: My Journey from Cancer, to Near Death, to True Healing.* Hay House, Inc., 2012.

AFTERWORD

1. Whether you're looking to expand on what you've learned, apply concepts with greater ease, or simply explore additional materials that complement your reading experience, our resource page is your gateway. Unlock a treasure trove of resources your journey by visiting today.
   https://www.upliftingeducation.com/resources

www.ingramcontent.com/pod-product-compliance
Lightning Source LLC
Chambersburg PA
CBHW040136160726

48006CB00014B/1516